1001 EVENTS
THAT MADE AMERICA

BY ALAN AXELROD

NATIONAL GEOGRAPHIC

WASHINGTON, DC

For Anita

Introduction

The modern English word "history" has its origin in the Greek word *historein*, meaning "to inquire," which, in turn, is derived from another Greek word, *histor*, meaning "learned man." These classical Greek words reached modern English by way of the Old French word *histoire*, but, just before the road they took ended at our language, it forked. While the English branch delivered a word that primarily means a narrative or story of past events, the French-bound version came to mean a narrative or story. Period.

If we follow the English-language branch, "history" strongly implies a narrative that is true: absolute nonfiction. If we take the French branch, we find no such claim, because an *histoire* is just a story, whether entirely factual, wholly fictitious, or a little of both.

"The very ink with which all history is written," Mark Twain wrote, "is merely fluid prejudice." That may be a bit too pessimistic, but, in all candor, we have to admit that the reality of history—the concept, not the word—is to be found along a road that unwinds somewhere between *history*-as-absolute-nonfiction and *histoire*-as-a-story. The fact is that all history is a story—an interpretation, a presentation, and an ordering—intended to be true, but, of course, shaped and filtered by whoever tells the tale. At best, then, history, narrative history, is an imperfect lens focused imperfectly on the past, full of scratches, cloudiness, blurs, and distortions.

But what's the alternative? A bare-bones timeline? A naked list of events? If we take away the story and just make a simple list, is this the equivalent of producing an unfiltered, undistorted lens?

Probably not. Timelines are pretty dull and deliver little understanding. In fact, few things carry less meaning than simple lists of names and dates. "1775–1783, American Revolution"—What does that mean?

In *1001 Events That Made America*, I take a third approach. Just as history is located between "history" and "histoire," this book moves between narrative and chronology, taking the best of both. I identify and isolate events beginning with the earliest peopling of America about 40,000 years ago and ending with the Enron convictions in 2006, but instead of merely listing these events, I tell a little story about each of them—usually no more than 50 words in length, sometimes even less, occasionally a little more, but always just enough (I hope) to outline the event, to explain its importance for American history, and perhaps to suggest how it is related to other important events.

While 1001 events are a lot of events, 40,000-plus years of history are a lot of years. So how did I happen to choose these particular 1001 events? And, for that matter, who do I think I am to have chosen them?

Maybe it's best to take the second question first. I am a student of American history. That means I've read a lot of American history and even written some myself. But more to the point, I am a person who thinks it's important to know who I am. For me, that means knowing where I came from, so that I can get a better idea of where I'm at, where I'm headed, and where I'm likely to end up. The surest way to this knowledge is through history, the collective stories of others through the centuries and the years who have both shaped and shared my country.

Now, how did I choose the events in this book?

Because I read a lot of history, I have a good idea of what most people who think and write about history believe is important to know about. Most of the events included in this book, therefore, represent the consensus of historians on just what events stand as genuine American landmarks—the events that shaped the nation and, therefore, the events we should know about because they tell us who we are and how we got that way. Because I also write history, however, I always try to look a little beyond the consensus and include some events that, as an American, speak directly to me. These include events from our nation's cultural and pop-cultural life, sports, entertainment, and art, as well as what a schoolteacher might call straight history. Whatever they are, if the events speak of America eloquently enough to me, I can only assume that they are important enough to pass on to you. Finally, because I am a human being, proud of a natural human urge to take count and keep score, I have also included among the 1001 events a generous helping of "firsts," "biggests," "greatests," and "worsts."

Now, there is one more question to ask and answer:

What should you do with this book? Should you read it from start to finish? Should you skim and skip around in it? Or should you start from the end and work backwards?

The correct answer is it doesn't really matter. If you're a person who enjoys seeing things grow, start from the beginning. If you prefer to start at the leaf tops and dig down to the roots, start from the end and work your way back. If you'd rather dip your hand into the river of time in various places, upstream, down, and up again, just browse. You won't get lost.

However you decide to read this book, you will find many people, many ideas, and many events, some that are familiar and some that aren't. But they all have one quality in common. They are 1001 things about America you really should know about. Some of the events are great, some good, some bad, beautiful, or ugly. But I believe that knowing about them—all of them—brings us closer to our country and our nation. This knowledge is the stuff of patriotism. — Alan Axelrod

About 40,000 B.C.

BEGINNING ABOUT 40,000 years ago, Asian peoples migrate from Siberia to Alaska over the solid tundra plain of the Bering Land Bridge, which existed where the 55-mile-wide Bering Strait lies today. Over thousands of years, the descendants of these people populate the Americas as far south as Tierra del Fuego at the tip of South America.

5500 B.C.

THE ANASAZI (a modern Navajo word meaning "Ancient Ones") create settlements in the American Southwest. The ancestors of the Native American peoples of the region, the Anasazi build spectacular cliff dwellings the Spanish invaders later call pueblos, meaning "towns," "villages," or "people." They also weave baskets of great beauty and, for that reason, are today sometimes referred to as the "Basket Weavers."

1000 B.C. – after A.D. 1500

NATIVE AMERICANS of various cultures build elaborate earthworks, the remains of which are found today from the Great Lakes to the Gulf of Mexico. Today known as the "Mound Builders," they left works ranging from vast burial mounds to temple mounds to circular and geometric ceremonial earthworks. The largest and most elaborate surviving structures are those of the Hopewell people (named for the mounds near Hopewell, Ohio), built in southern Ohio by an agricultural and trading community that flourished mainly from 300 BC to AD 700.

About A.D. 1000

THE VIKING captain Leif Eriksson spends a winter exploring part of Newfoundland from "Vinland" (named for its abundance of grapes or berries), a rude settlement he establishes there, at a place now called L'Anse aux Meadows. In 986, another Norseman, Bjarni Herjulfsson, had sighted Newfoundland, but Eriksson is the first European to go ashore in North America, look around, and build a few huts.

1007

THORFINN KARLSEFNI (who is probably Leif Eriksson's brother) occupies Vinland (on Newfoundland) for about two years. While here, his wife, Gudrid, gives birth to the first Euro-American child, a son named Snorro.

1492

OCTOBER 12 — Cristoforo Colombo, a Genoese mariner sailing under the patronage of Queen Isabella and King Ferdinand I of Spain—and known to them as Cristóbal Colón, but to Americans as Christopher Columbus—journeys across the Atlantic in search of a short route to gold-and-spice-rich Asia. He finds instead, on October 12, a Caribbean island the natives call Guanahani and which he names San Salvador.

1493

JANUARY 16 — After completing his first voyage, Columbus departs on his return voyage to Spain, leaving behind a 39-man garrison on the island he calls Hispaniola (today divided between Haiti and the Dominican Republic). In his absence, Columbus's men rape and pillage the local inhabitants, who retaliate by wiping out the entire garrison. It is the first war between whites and "Indians" (as Columbus calls the Native Americans) in the New World.

1507

THE GERMAN geographer Martin Waldseemüller coins the name "America" in his *Cosmographiae Introductio,* mistakenly attributing the discovery of the New World to the Italian navigator Amerigo Vespucci (Americus Vesupuccius), who did not sail to the New World until 1499 or 1497 at the earliest, at least five years after Columbus.

1513

APRIL 2 — While searching for what natives have told him is a miraculous "fountain of youth," Juan Ponce de León claims Florida for the king of Spain.

1526

LEADING 500 – 600 settlers from Hispaniola to the coast of South Carolina (probably just north of the mouth of the Peedee River) in the early summer, the Spaniard Lucas Vazquez de Ayllón establishes San Miguel de Guadalupe, the first European settlement in what is now the United States. Within months, Ayllón and all but 150 others succumb to fever. The survivors return to Hispaniola on October 18.

1540

FRANCISCO CORONADO treks through Kansas with some 260 horses, most of which get away from him and range throughout the Midwest as far south as Mexico and as far north as Canada. These animals become the ancestors of the American wild horse as later generations of them interbreed with the horses of Norman stock brought by the French explorers and settlers of Canada during the 17th and early 18th centuries.

1540–1542

MOTIVATED BY Native American stories about "Cibola" and its "Seven Cities of Gold" and hoping to reap a bonanza of New World wealth (as Hernan Cortés had done among the Aztecs of Mexico), Francisco Coronado explores much of the American lower Midwest and Southwest. After two years, he returns to Mexico and the court of Spanish viceroy Antonio de Mendoza empty handed.

1541

MAY 8 — Members of Hernando de Soto's conquistador band become the first Europeans to see the Mississippi River.

1562

APRIL 30 — Seeking refuge from religious persecution in France, Huguenots (French Protestants) led by Jean Ribaut establish Port Royal on Parris Island, off the coast of South Carolina. They are the first French colonists in what will become the United States; however, the colony dissolves in 1564 when promised supplies fail to arrive.

1565

ENGLISH SLAVE trader John Hawkins visits a French colony in Florida and is introduced to smoking tobacco by colonists, who have in turn acquired the habit from Native Americans. Hawkins hauls a shipload of tobacco back to England, claiming that the "smoke satisfieth... hunger" so that one may go "foure or five days without meat or drinke."

SEPTEMBER 8 — Spanish naval officer Pedro Menéndez de Avilés founds St. Augustine, in northern Florida on the coast of the Atlantic Ocean, the first permanent European colony in America.

LATE SEPTEMBER — Seeking to drive off rival French colonists in northern Florida, the Spaniard Pedro Menéndez de Avilés leads an attack on Fort Caroline, a French stronghold, and kills its garrison. Renamed San Mateo, it becomes the first of a string of Spanish forts that eventually stretches all the way to Tampa Bay. The New World is now a battlefield for competing Old World interests.

1566

UNDER THE sponsorship of Pedro Menéndez de Avilés, the first three Jesuit missionaries arrive in what will become the United States. They establish themselves in Guale (in present-day Georgia) and in Orista and Santa Elena (in modern South Carolina). Local natives soon force them to leave.

1579

SAILING FOR Queen Elizabeth I, the British sea dog Francis
Drake circumnavigates the globe, stopping long enough
just north of present-day San Francisco to lay claim to
the territory of California as "New Albion" ("Albion" is
an archaic and poetic name for England). England fails to
develop the claim, and California later becomes a possession of the Spanish crown.

1585–1590

IN A VAST territory he names Virginia to honor England's
"Virgin Queen," Elizabeth I, courtier Sir Walter Raleigh
sponsors an English colony on Roanoke Island, in what is
today North Carolina's Outer Banks. Established in
August 1585, it is quickly abandoned. Another 150
colonists, under John White, arrive to reestablish the settlement in July 1587. White sets sail for England on
August 25 to fetch more supplies, but his return to the
colony is delayed by war with Spain. When he belatedly
reaches Roanoke on August 17, 1590, he discovers the
colony utterly vanished, except for the single word
"Croatoan" carved into a tree. White takes the carving to
mean that the colonists had moved to an island, called
Croatoan, about 50 miles away, but no trace of the "Lost
Colony" is ever found, and the fate of some 150 men,
women, and children remains unknown.

1587

AUGUST 18 — Virginia Dare is born to Ananias and Ellinor
Dare on Roanoke Island. The first English child to be born

in America, Virginia vanishes with the other inhabitants of the Lost Colony.

1607

MAY 14 — Jamestown, Virginia, is founded, first permanent English colony in what will become the United States.

1607

DECEMBER — While on a foraging expedition, Capt. John Smith, military leader of the Jamestown colony, is captured by members of a tribe led by the venerable sachem (chief) known to the English as Powhatan. As Smith relates the story, his captors are about to beat out his brains when he is saved by the intercession of Powhatan's 12-year-old daughter, Pocahontas. The romantic vignette of Smith's rescue enters into American legend and lore, but, more importantly, Pocahontas goes on to become a peacemaker between the English and her people.

1608

CAPT. JOHN SMITH'S *A True Relation of Such Occurrences and Accidents of Noate as Hath Hapned in Virginia Since the First Planting of that Colony,* is published in London and generally considered to be the first American book.

1609

SAILING IN the Half Moon, Henry Hudson, an English mariner working for the Dutch, explores the river and

ESTIMATED COLONIAL POPULATION: 210

great bay that come to bear his name, vainly searching for the "Northwest Passage," the fabled waterway believed to connect the Atlantic Ocean to the Pacific. The Hudson River and Hudson Bay became two of early America's key waterways, but Hudson himself falls victim to a mutiny and, on June 12, 1611, is cast adrift on Hudson Bay, never to be heard from again.

1609–1610

WINTER — Jamestown, Virginia endures the "Starving Time," a brutal winter in which half the colony dies. The arrival on June 10, 1610, of the dictatorial Royal Governor Thomas West De La Warr brings an improvement in the colony's fortunes.

1616

VAST NUMBERS of Native Americans die in a smallpox epidemic. Brought by incoming colonists, the contagion almost completely wipes out the tribes of upper New England.

1619

A DUTCH ship carrying 20 African slaves lands at Jamestown, Virginia, offering its cargo for sale. These are the first African slaves sold in America and the beginning of slavery in America.

JULY 30 — Virginia's House of Burgesses, the first legislative body to convene in America, meets in Jamestown's Old Church.

1620

NOVEMBER 21 — After crossing the Atlantic Ocean from England, Colonists riding at anchor in Provincetown Harbor, Massachusetts, in the ship *Mayflower* draw up the "Mayflower Compact," an agreement between the Puritan Separatists (later popularly known as "Pilgrims") and the non-Puritan colonists (whom the Pilgrims call "Strangers"). The two groups of colonists agree to combine "ourselves together into a civill body politick" and pledge to work together "for the generall good of the Colonie." Signed by 41 colonists aboard the *Mayflower,* this is the first constitution written in and for people of North America.

DECEMBER 26 — The Pilgrims and Strangers aboard the *Mayflower* land at Plymouth, Massachusetts, and disembark. According to legend, they set foot on what is later called "Plymouth Rock," which is now preserved, inscribed with year 1620, at Plymouth.

1621

THE PILGRIMS and local Wampanoag Indians conclude a treaty of peace and defensive alliance at Strawberry Hill, Plymouth, Massachusetts. Brokered by Squanto, an English-speaking Indian who befriends the Pilgrims, this is the first treaty between whites and Native Americans. The harvest meal the Pilgrims share with the Wampanoag in the autumn of this year is cited by some historians as the model for the modern Thanksgiving holiday.

1622

MARCH 22 — Chief Powhatan's brother, Opechancanough, attacks white settlements outside of Jamestown, Virginia, nearly destroying all of them. Jamestown itself, heavily fortified, resists this first "Indian massacre" of white colonists.

1622–1646

OPECHANCANOUGH LEADS the so-called Powhatan Confederacy (at least 32 tribes in the vicinity of Jamestown, Virginia) in sporadic warfare that ends, after many deaths on both sides, with a peace treaty in October 1646.

1624

MAY — Cornelius J. Mey leads 30 families to the shore of what is now New York Bay and founds the Dutch colony of New Netherland two years later.

1626

AUGUST 10 — Peter Minuit, director-general of New Netherland, purchases Manhattan Island from the Manhattan Indians (a branch of the Delaware tribe) for trade goods valued at 60 Dutch guilders, which a 19th-century American historian later computes as the equivalent of $24.

1630

JUNE 30 — John Winthrop enters Salem Harbor with 900 Puritan refugees from England and founds the Massachusetts Bay Colony, destined to become a larger and more influential Puritan colony than the Pilgrims' Plymouth, which it absorbs in 1691.

1630

SEPTEMBER 30 — John Billington, a Pilgrim, is hanged for murder. He is the first criminal to suffer capital punishment in the American colonies.

1632

JUNE 20 — Cecilius Calvert, second Lord Baltimore, is granted a royal charter to found Maryland. It becomes a haven for Roman Catholics, who are persecuted in New England as well as old England.

1635

SEPTEMBER 13 — Radical minister Roger Williams is banished from the Massachusetts Bay Colony. In June 1636, Williams founds the colony of Rhode Island (on land legally purchased from local Native Americans) on the principles of the separation of church and state ("Coerced religion stinks in God's nostrils," he declares) and religious tolerance.

1636

OCTOBER 28 — Harvard College, the first college in America, is founded in a single frame house and "college yard" at Cambridge, Massachusetts, for the purpose of educating young men for the Puritan clergy.

1637

NOVEMBER 7 — Anne Hutchinson is banished from the Massachusetts Bay Colony for preaching her belief that

ESTIMATED COLONIAL POPULATION: 4,646

faith, not strict adherence to any body of orthodox theology, is sufficient for salvation. She settles in Roger Williams's Rhode Island and is today regarded as a champion of liberty, freedom of religion, and even an early form of feminism.

1637–1638

SPRING — The Massachusetts Bay and Plymouth colonies declare war on the Pequot Indians in an effort to gain new territory. After the tribe is virtually wiped out, the Treaty of Hartford (September 21, 1638) ends the war.

1638

SWEDISH COLONISTS in Delaware introduce the log cabin (of Finnish origin) to America.

1638–1684

THE IROQUOIS tribes (Mohawk, Oneida, Onondaga, Cayuga, and Seneca), which occupy territory extending from the Hudson Valley in the east to Lake Ontario in the west, conduct a long series of wars against the Huron and other tribes in an effort to monopolize the fur trade by usurping hunting grounds rich with beaver. For this reason, these intertribal conflicts are collectively known as the Beaver Wars.

1639–1645

NEW NETHERLAND governor Willem Kieft wages war against the Algonquin tribes in and around his colony. During the night of February 25–26, 1643, he perpetrates a horrific massacre of Wappinger Indians—men, women, and children—at Pavonia (modern Jersey City), New Jersey. This provokes massive tribal retaliation, and New Amsterdam (modern New York City) finds itself in a virtual state of siege for more than a year.

1640

THE WHOLE *Booke of Psalmes Faithfully Translated into English Metre,* familiarly called the *Bay Psalm Book,* published in Cambridge, Massachusetts, is the first book printed in America.

1641

OCTOBER — The first American patent is issued by the Massachusetts Bay Colony to Samuel Winslow of Massachusetts for a salt-making process.

1644–1654

WHILE THE Civil War rages in England, colonial Catholic supporters of King Charles I and colonial Protestant partisans of Oliver Cromwell fight one another in what becomes known as Maryland's Religious War. The war ends with the Battle of the Severn on March 25, 1654, as a result of which the victorious Protestants gain a measure of control over Maryland's government. Maryland's Religious War is America's first civil war.

1648

JANUARY 21 — Margaret Brent appeals to the Maryland Assembly with a request that, as a property holder, she be granted the right to vote. Although Governor Thomas Greene denies her petition, Brent is nevertheless considered the first American woman suffragist.

1648–1650

EAGER TO suppress French trade competition, Dutch traders at Fort Orange (modern Albany, New York) supply their Iroquois trading partners with guns and ammunition to enable them to invade the territory of the Huron, who are trading partners of the French. The Huron are decimated in the course of this white-supported intertribal conflict.

1650

THE TENTH Muse Lately Sprung Up in America, a volume of poems on religion and life in Puritan New England by Anne Bradstreet of Massachusetts, is published in London, making Bradstreet the first published American poet.

1652

JUNE 10 — In defiance of English colonial law, the first American mint is established in Boston and produces the celebrated "Pine Tree" shilling, designed by the mint's master, silversmith John Hull.

1654

JULY 8 — Jacob Barsimon leaves Holland, arriving in Manhattan on May 22. He is the first Jew to settle in America.

ESTIMATED COLONIAL POPULATION: 26,634

1659

OCTOBER 27 — Having banished all Quakers, pursuant to a law of May 29, 1658, Massachusetts authorities hang, on Boston Common, two Quakers foolish enough to return to the colony.

1660

JOHN ELIOT establishes the first Indian church in North America at Natick, Massachusetts, a village he had founded in 1657 as a place of residence for Christianized Native Americans, called "praying Indians."

DECEMBER 1 — The British Parliament reenacts the first Navigation Act, originally passed in 1651, imposing numerous restrictions on colonial trade. For nearly a century, this and subsequent acts regulating colonial trade are not enforced; when King George III decides to enforce them in the mid-1770s, he stirs the colonies to revolution.

1661

SEPTEMBER — King Charles II, a friend of Quaker leader William Penn, orders Massachusetts governor John Endicott to call a halt to the persecution of Quakers in his colony.

1662

MARCH — A synod of Massachusetts churches adopts the "Half-Way Covenant," permitting parents who have been

ESTIMATED COLONIAL POPULATION: 50,368

baptized but who no longer profess the faith to have their children baptized. This relaxation of strict Puritan Congregationalist practice is a telltale sign of the diminishment of the influence of Puritanism, formerly dominant in New England.

1664

MARYLAND PASSES a Slavery Act that fully sanctions lifelong servitude for black slaves. The act is designed to prevent slaves from gaining freedom by accepting baptism in the Christian church.

FALL — New York governor Richard Nicolls establishes the Newmarket Course at Hempstead Plains, Long Island, and holds horse races, the first organized sport in America. Nicolls also writes the rules and posts the prizes.

SEPTEMBER 7 — Peter Stuyvesant, Dutch governor of New Netherland, surrenders his colony to an English naval force under Col. Richard Nicolls. New Netherland is reorganized under English rule as the colonies of New Jersey and New York, and New Amsterdam is renamed New York City.

1665

YE BARE and Ye Cub by Philip Alexander Bruce is the first play staged in America, at Acomac, Virginia.

ESTIMATED COLONIAL POPULATION: 75,058

1673

FATHER JACQUES MARQUETTE and Louis Jolliet explore the Mississippi River, preparing the way for French colonization of the continent between the Appalachians and the Rocky Mountains.

1675–1676

KING PHILIP'S War rages between most of white New England and the Wampanoag and their allied tribes, led by Chief Metacomet, whom the colonists derisively call King Philip. In proportion to the white and Indian population of New England at the time, it is the deadliest war in American history.

1676

IN BACON'S REBELLION, Virginia demagogue Nathaniel Bacon leads disgruntled Virginia frontier settlers in an unauthorized war against local Indians and an uprising against the royal governor, Sir William Berkeley, and the House of Burgesses (colonial assembly). The revolt is most important historically as an early conflict between the struggling frontier (the "Piedmont") and the moneyed establishment of the coast (the "Tidewater").

1677

FOR HIS colony of West New Jersey, William Penn drafts the first American charter legally guaranteeing separation of church and state. (In 1636, Roger Williams

ESTIMATED COLONIAL POPULATION: 111,935

established a similar political principle for Rhode Island, but embodied no binding guarantee in a charter or constitution.)

1680

AUGUST 10 — The Tewa medicine man Popé leads a brilliantly planned and executed revolt among the Native American pueblos of the Spanish Southwest, culminating in the invasion of Santa Fe (New Mexico) on August 15. The Spanish do not regain control of Santa Fe until 1692 and of all the pueblos until some four years after that.

1681

MARCH 4 — England's King Charles II grants the territory roughly encompassing the modern state of Pennsylvania ("Penn's Woods") to William Penn, a Quaker who already has proprietary interests in New Jersey.

1687

AFTER ENGLAND's King James II decides to consolidate the New England colonies, Royal Governor Edmund Andros dissolves the colonial assemblies and demands the surrender of all colonial charters. The Connecticut charter, granted in 1662, mysteriously disappears, however, having been hidden by Capt. Joseph Wadsworth in the hollow of a white oak tree. This tree, which comes to be known as the "Charter Oak," is said to be

ESTIMATED COLONIAL POPULATION: 151,507

1,000 years old and continues to stand until 1856. The Charter Oak long figures as a symbol of righteous rebellion in America.

1689–1691

IN LEISLER'S Rebellion, Jacob Leisler leads New York farmers and merchants in an uprising against Catholics and suspected Catholics in the English colonial administration. Leisler is hanged as a traitor on May 16, 1691, but the movement he has begun persists for years as a powerful anti-Catholic and anti-aristocratic force in the New York colony.

1689–1697

KING WILLIAM'S War, fought between the English and Iroquois (mostly Mohawk) on one side and the French and Abenaki Indians on the other, is the North American theater of Europe's War of the Grand Alliance (also called the War of the League of Augsburg or the Nine Years' War). In America, the war is fought to gain control of trade and territory.

1690

MASSACHUSETTS PRINTS the first paper currency in America and uses it to pay soldiers who are fighting in King William's War.

SEPTEMBER 25 — Printer-editor Benjamin Harris begins publication of *Publick Occurrences* in Boston. The first newspaper in the colonies, it lasts just four days before royal officials put an end to it because Harris failed to secure official permission to start the paper.

1692–1697

FEBRUARY 1692 — Two young daughters of the Reverend Samuel Parrish and some of their friends, all of whom are behaving in an unruly manner, are diagnosed by a Salem, Massachusetts, physician as being under the spell of a witch. Confronted with the diagnosis, the girls make accusations, and the Salem witch hunt and witch trials begin. They do not officially end until 1697, by which time 19 convicted witches have been hanged and one man, Giles Corey, has been pressed to death under stones for refusing to stand trial.

1695

THE PIMA INDIANS of lower Pimeria Alta (Sonora, Mexico, and southern Arizona) rebel against the Spanish. The uprising is quickly put down.

NEW YORK CITY appoints official overseers to administer public relief to the poor. Clothing supplied to paupers bears a red or blue cloth badge with "N.Y." emblazoned on it.

1701

THE VESTRY ACT makes Anglicanism the state religion of North Carolina, which had been founded in 1663 without mention of religion.

ESTIMATED COLONIAL POPULATION: 210,372

1702–1713

QUEEN ANNE'S WAR, the American theater of the European War of the Spanish Succession, is fought between the English colonies and the French colonies (with Indian allies on both sides). It ends with the Treaty of Utrecht on July 13, 1713, which also ends the European war. Yet another struggle for dominance of North America, the war results in the French loss of Newfoundland, Hudson Bay, and Acadia (in Nova Scotia). French-allied Indians are compelled to swear allegiance to the British crown.

1711–1712

CHRONICALLY PERSECUTED and cheated by colonists in North Carolina, the Tuscarora Indians violently resist further white settlement. North and South Carolinian forces respond with a war that virtually destroys the tribe; survivors migrate north to New York and join the Iroquois "Five Nations" League as the league's sixth nation.

1715–1716

AFTER THE Yamasee of South Carolina retaliate against English colonists for abuses suffered and kill 100 colonists in a raid, South Carolinians join forces with the Cherokee to drive them from their lands in South Carolina, Georgia, and northern Florida. The colonists call this the Yamasee War.

ESTIMATED COLONIAL POPULATION: 250,888

1720

OCTOBER 20 — Scottish financier John Law's grandiose scheme to promote and finance French colonization in Louisiana becomes the "Mississippi Bubble" when the issuance of paper currency exceeds the availability of securities to back it. Thousands of prominent European investors are ruined, although the scheme does jump-start the colonization of Louisiana.

1722

THE POWERFUL Iroquois (Six Nations) League, centered in New York but often ranging throughout much of the Northeast, concludes a major treaty with Virginia, pledging not to cross the Potomac River or the Blue Ridge Mountains. The Iroquois tribes are the English colonies' most important Native American allies.

1725

THE FIRST separate church for "colored" Baptists is founded at Williamsburg, Virginia.

1729

NOVEMBER 28 — The Natchez Indians near the Mississippi city that today bears their name attack Fort Rosalie, killing some 200 French colonists. In response, the French launch a ruthless campaign against the Natchez and an allied tribe, the Yazoo. The number killed is not

ESTIMATED COLONIAL POPULATION: 331,711

known, but some 400 Natchez and Yazoo prisoners of war are sold into slavery in the West Indies.

1731

THE LIBRARY COMPANY of Philadelphia is founded by Benjamin Franklin as a circulating library, the very first in the world.

1732

THE FIRST American stagecoach line is established between the New Jersey towns of Burlington and Amboy.

JUNE 9 — King George II of England grants James Oglethorpe a royal charter to found Georgia chiefly as a refuge and fresh start for English debtors, who would otherwise be jailed in England. Hoping to create a New World utopia, Oglethorpe bans slavery and limits the amount of land any individual can own. Within a remarkably brief time, a ruling class nevertheless rises in the colony, seizes control of Georgia, and overturns both regulations.

1733

MAY 17 — The British Parliament passes the Molasses Act, which gives English producers a monopoly on rum and molasses production in the colonies. It is one in the series of restrictive trade laws that, collectively, create the colonial discontent leading to the American Revolution.

ESTIMATED COLONIAL POPULATION: 466,185

1735

OCTOBER 1734 — John Peter Zenger, publisher of the *New York Weekly Journal,* is arrested for "seditious libel" when he prints criticism of New York Governor William Cosby. Andrew Hamilton defends him at trial in 1735 and secures his acquittal on the grounds that the truth can never be deemed libelous. The decision is an American milestone in the principle of freedom of the press.

1737

AUGUST 25 — William Penn's son Thomas negotiates the "Walking Purchase" of land from the Delaware Indians, concluding an agreement to pace off land deeded to his father by the tribe. The deed encompasses all the land a man can walk across in a day and a half. Penn hires a team of professional walkers who, collectively, manage to pace off a total of 66.5 miles. The swindle sours the friendly relations between Pennsylvania and the Indians that William Penn had worked so vigorously to establish.

1739

SEPTEMBER 9 — Slaves from Charleston, South Carolina, set out for St. Augustine, Florida, believing the Spanish missionaries there will free them. Along the way, they kill 21 whites before they are surrounded and massacred. Forty-one slaves perish.

ESTIMATED COLONIAL POPULATION: **629,445**

1741

JULY 8 — Jonathan Edwards delivers a sermon entitled "Sinners in the Hands of an Angry God" to his congregation in Enfield, Massachusetts (now in Connecticut). The sermon represents the zenith of a religious revival, the "Great Awakening," which powerfully influences culture and politics as well as religion.

1742

DURING THE War of Jenkins's Ear (provoked by British outrage over an assault on a merchant captain who claims that Spanish colonial coastguardsmen cut off his ear), Spanish forces attack English colonists at Fort Frederica, on St. Simons Island off the Georgia coast. The English defeat the attackers at the Battle of Bloody Marsh on June 9. While the battle is decisive for the War of Jenkins's Ear, that smaller war soon dissolves into the four-year-long King George's War between Spain's ally France and England.

1743

A QUAKER, John Woolman, begins the first organized antislavery campaign in America by preaching against slavery throughout the colonies.

1744–1748

ONCE AGAIN, the French and British (each with Indian allies) fight for dominance in North America. King George's War is the American theater of the European War of the

ESTIMATED COLONIAL POPULATION: 905,563

Austrian Succession. The Treaty of Aix-la-Chapelle ends both the American and European wars, undoing many of the gains the English colonists had made against the French as a result of the earlier Queen Anne's War.

1751

BENJAMIN FRANKLIN earns international fame as a scientist with his *Experiments and Observations in Electricity* and as an economist with *Observations Concerning the Increase of Mankind.* As a figure of international renown, he will go on to become a key diplomat during and after the American Revolution.

NOVEMBER 20 — A Pima named Oacpicagigua leads the Second Pima Revolt against the Spanish, 50 years after the first revolt. The Pima, Papago, and Sobipuri Indians attack missions and ranches in the Southwest. Oacpicagigua hopes to unite the Indians in a genuine revolution, but alliances dissolve, and the Spanish quickly defeat the rebels.

1754–1763

THE FRENCH and Indian War, the North American theater of the Seven Years' War (which engulfs Europe and European colonial possessions in the Caribbean, India, Asia, and the Pacific), becomes the final contest between the French (and their numerous Indian allies, plus Spain) and the English (with fewer Indian allies) for dominance of the continent. The French are initially successful, but

ESTIMATED COLONIAL POPULATION: **1,170,760**

the war ends disastrously for them, and France yields to Britain in America.

1754

MAY 28 — George Washington, a 22-year-old Virginia militia colonel, is victorious in a minor backwoods skirmish against a party of French soldiers and officials in Pennsylvania that ignites the titanic French and Indian War.

JULY 4 — An outnumbered George Washington is defeated at the Battle of Great Meadows in Pennsylvania. The French seize control of the vast Ohio country west of the Appalachians.

1758

OCTOBER — After suffering a series of defeats at the hands of the French and their Indian allies, the British conclude the Treaty of Easton with Indian tribes in western Pennsylvania, thereby depriving the French of some of their most important allies and turning the tide of the French and Indian War in favor of the British.

1763

MAY 7 — The Ottawa Indian chief Pontiac raids the fort at Detroit, beginning "Pontiac's Rebellion," a violent coda to the French and Indian War and a last-ditch attempt by the tribes of the upper Midwest to end white settlement on their land. The war continues for three years, ending in 1766 with the exhaustion of Pontiac and his followers.

OCTOBER 7 — Hoping to end warfare between English colonists and Indians by stopping white incursion into Indian lands, King George III issues a proclamation setting the Appalachian Mountains as the western limit of English settlement. The "Proclamation of 1763" brings temporary peace with some Indian tribes, but it outrages frontier settlers, who continue to freely cross the line. Many historians see this defiance as the seed of the American Revolution.

1765

WITH HIS portrait of John Hancock, John Singleton Copley emerges as America's first painter of international reputation.

MARCH 22 AND 24 — The British Parliament passes the Stamp Act and Quartering Act. The first requires the purchase of government stamps to be affixed to documents, stationery, and other paper products (including playing cards). The second requires the colonies to supply housing or quarters for British soldiers at public expense. Both acts outrage a growing faction of colonists, deepening alienation from the government of the mother country.

MAY 29 — Virginia legislator Patrick Henry attacks the Stamp Act in a fiery speech before the House of Burgesses. To shouts of "Treason!" he responds famously: "If this be treason, make the most of it!"

ESTIMATED COLONIAL POPULATION: 1,593,625

OCTOBER 7–25 — The Stamp Act Congress, attended by 28 delegates from nine colonies, meets in New York City to fashion a united response to Parliament and the king. The pattern will prove characteristic: Each repressive British law produces greater colonial unity.

1766

MARCH 17 — In response to a colonial boycott of English goods initiated by the Stamp Act Congress, London merchants successfully petition Parliament for repeal of the act.

MARCH 18 — The very day it repeals the Stamp Act, Parliament passes the Declaratory Act, affirming that Parliament may establish laws that are binding on the colonies.

1767

DANIEL BOONE probes the Cumberland Gap in the Appalachians, the first step in opening Kentucky—and the West—to settlement.

RESPONDING TO complaints of arrogance, brutality, and tyranny, the Spanish Crown expels the powerful Jesuit missionaries from its New World settlements ("New Spain") and replaces them with the more humane Franciscans, who begin to establish a system of economically, culturally, and politically vital and influential missions throughout the Southwest.

JUNE 29 — Parliament passes the Townshend Revenue Act, requiring colonists to pay duties on tea, glass, painter's colors, lead, and paper. It is the first of the so-called Townshend Acts (named after Chancellor of the Exchequer Charles Townshend), which impose on the colonies what influential colonists see as unjust taxes.

1768

SEPTEMBER 28 — British warships drop anchor in Boston Harbor. On October 1, two regiments of Redcoats debark in Boston to enforce order in increasingly unruly New England. However, the quartering of the troops in Boston serves only to increase revolutionary discontent.

1769

FRANCISCAN MISSIONARY Junipero Serra founds the first California mission, San Diego de Alcala (at modern San Diego). Over the next 15 years, Serra establishes eight more missions along the Camino Real (King's Highway) north to San Francisco Bay. These become the first permanent Euro-American settlements in California.

1770

MARCH 5 — A confrontation between British troops and colonists erupts into a riot called the "Boston Massacre." Five Bostonians are killed, including a fugitive slave, Crispus Attucks, who is traditionally remembered as the first casualty in the colonies' struggle for independence. Capt. Thomas Preston and six of his men are indicted for murder, but are ably defended by colonists John Adams and Josiah Quincy, who thereby avert mob "justice"; two are found guilty of manslaughter, the rest acquitted.

APRIL 12 — Bowing to colonial discontent, Parliament repeals all of the odious Townshend Acts, except for the tax on tea.

1771

BENJAMIN FRANKLIN begins work on his autobiography. Although never completed and not published until after his death, the book presents Franklin as the embodiment—and example to other Americans—of all that is possible in America if one is alert, works hard, and remains open to opportunity. It is a classic American story.

1773

APRIL 27 — Parliament passes the Tea Act, designed to bolster the faltering East India Company by effectively giving it a monopoly on tea imports to the colonies at the expense of American tea merchants.

DECEMBER 16 — A group of militant Bostonians respond to the Tea Act by dressing as Indians, boarding three British tea ships in Boston Harbor, and throwing tea valued at £18,000 overboard. The "Boston Tea Party" galvanizes colonial opposition to the Crown's continued policy of regulating colonial commerce and taxing the colonies, which are not represented in Parliament.

1774

MARCH 31 — Parliament passes the first of what it calls the Coercive Acts and the colonists call the Intolerable Acts.

ESTIMATED COLONIAL POPULATION: 2,148,079

Intended to punish the residents of Boston for the Boston Tea Party, the first act closes the city's port. Subsequent acts passed on May 20 sharply restrict public meetings and give the Crown, not the colony, jurisdiction over capital offenses charged against British officials.

JUNE 2 AND JUNE 22 — Two more of the Intolerable Acts are passed: The Quartering Act is restored and extended; it now requires private citizens to house and feed British troops. The Quebec Act assigns to British-controlled, French-speaking Quebec land claimed by the English-speaking colonies.

SEPTEMBER 17 — The First Continental Congress meets and approves the Suffolk Resolves. Originally passed by a convention in Suffolk County, Massachusetts, the resolves call for united and organized resistance to force the repeal of the Intolerable Acts.

1775–1783

THE AMERICAN REVOLUTION is fought, ultimately leading to the establishment of an independent United States of America.

1775

APRIL 19 — The first actual battles of the American Revolution are fought in Massachusetts at Lexington and Concord. The Americans are defeated at Lexington, but prevail at Concord, forcing British troops to withdraw—under deadly sniper fire all the way—to quarters in Boston.

MAY 10 — The Second Continental Congress convenes in Philadelphia.

JUNE 17 — The Battle of Bunker Hill—actually fought on adjacent Breed's Hill above Boston—ends when American forces withdraw, having lost the hill but also having inflicted very heavy casualties on the stunned British army.

JULY 15 — The Second Continental Congress creates the Continental Army and names George Washington to command it.

1776

JANUARY 10 — Colonial debate continues on whether to seek outright independence. Thomas Paine, a recent English immigrant to Philadelphia, publishes a pamphlet called *Common Sense,* which dramatically makes the case for independence and sways the debate in its favor.

MARCH 17 — Surrounded by American forces, the British army evacuates Boston and withdraws by ship all the way to Halifax, Nova Scotia.

JULY 4 — The Continental Congress approves the Declaration of Independence, drafted by Thomas Jefferson and edited by members of the Congress. The congressional delegates sign the document on August 2.

SEPTEMBER 6 — David Bushnell's primitive one-man submarine, *Turtle,* attacks British admiral Richard Howe's flagship in New York Bay. This raid—history's first submarine attack by history's first submarine—fails, as does a second one later in the month.

SEPTEMBER 9 — The Continental Congress officially creates the name "United States of America."

SEPTEMBER 22 — Capt. Nathan Hale, a Connecticut schoolmaster, is hanged as a spy in New York City by the British. His last words are "I only regret that I have but one life to lose for my country."

DECEMBER 5 — The Phi Beta Kappa fraternity is founded at the College of William and Mary, Williamsburg, Virginia. The first American college fraternity, its membership consists of five students.

DECEMBER 25 – 26 — Having lost New York City to the British and after retreating across New Jersey into Pennsylvania, Gen. George Washington recrosses the Delaware River to triumph against elite Hessian mercenaries at the Battle of Trenton. The battle revives the faltering fortunes of the American forces.

1777

JANUARY 3 — Washington caps his victory at Trenton with a triumph at Princeton, New Jersey.

AUGUST 16 — Fighting under General John Stark, American forces defeat General John Burgoyne's British and Hessian troops at the Battle of Bennington (Vermont), killing 200 and capturing 600.

SEPTEMBER 19 AND OCTOBER 7 — American forces are victorious against the British troops of "Gentleman Johnny" Burgoyne near Saratoga, New York (in the Battle of Freeman's Farm, September 19, and Battle of Bemis Heights, October 7).

SEPTEMBER 26 — While Burgoyne is being defeated at Saratoga, British general William Howe takes Philadelphia, seat of the Continental Congress. (The Congress has fled.)

OCTOBER 4 — In an effort to recover from the loss of Philadelphia, Gen. George Washington fights aggressively at the Battle of Germantown. He loses, but his audacity, resolve, courage, and leadership so impress French observers that they persuade Emperor Louis XVI to make a full and formal alliance with the Americans. The alliance proves instrumental in achieving ultimate victory.

NOVEMBER 15 — The Continental Congress adopts the Articles of Confederation, which, after they are ratified in 1781, serve as the national constitution until the passage of an entirely new constitution on December 7, 1787.

1778

FEBRUARY 6 — Three separate but related treaties of military alliance with France are concluded.

1779

SEPTEMBER 23 — The dashing American naval commander John Paul Jones defeats HMS *Serapis,* one of many remarkable victories he achieves in battle against the world's most powerful naval force.

1780

MARCH 1 — Pennsylvania becomes the first state to abolish slavery. The New England states follow, beginning in 1784.

SEPTEMBER 23 — The capture of British major John André reveals the treachery of turncoat American general Benedict Arnold, who has secretly offered to surrender the key Hudson River fort at West Point to the British. André is hanged on October 2. Arnold flees to the British lines and becomes a general in the enemy army.

OCTOBER 7 — After suffering a humiliating defeat in the South at Camden, South Carolina, on August 16, American forces score a spectacular victory at King's Mountain, South Carolina, killing 150 and taking some 800 prisoners.

1781

OCTOBER 19 — Lord Charles Cornwallis surrenders his army to a Franco-American force under George Washington and French general Comte de Rochambeau at the Battle of Yorktown, Virginia. Although a definitive peace treaty

ESTIMATED U.S. POPULATION: 2,780,369

is not signed until 1783, this victory ensures the success of the revolution and is its last large battle.

1783

NOAH WEBSTER publishes *The American Spelling Book,* a landmark in the history of the American language.

SEPTEMBER 3 — British and American negotiators (including Benjamin Franklin, John Jay, John Adams, and Henry Laurens) conclude the Treaty of Paris, ending the American Revolution and securing American independence.

1785

THE STATE of Virginia authorizes the Little River Turnpike, the first government-funded highway in the nation.

JULY 6 — Thomas Jefferson proposes a decimal coinage system based on the Spanish milled dollar. Congress makes the dollar the basis of U.S. currency on August 8.

1786

RESPONDING TO economic depression, high taxes, and a wave of frontier property foreclosures, Massachusetts farmer Daniel Shays leads "Shays's Rebellion" against the courts and other officials in western Massachusetts. Under the Articles of Confederation ratified five years earlier, the weak federal government is powerless to step in and restore order. Massachusetts governor James Bowdoin appeals to Boston merchants to finance a force of 4,400 volunteers, and the uprising is finally put down.

Fear of future rebellions generates support for a convention to draw up a stronger constitution to replace the Articles.

THE PRINTERS of Philadelphia call a strike—the first recorded organized labor strike in America. They attain their objective: a wage of $6 per week.

AUGUST 7 — Congress passes the first Federal Indian Act, creating two federally regulated Indian "departments," one north of the Ohio River, the other south of it.

1786–1794

THE SHAWNEE chief Blue Jacket and the Miami chief Little Turtle lead Shawnee, Miami, Ottawa, and other tribes in a war against whites attempting to settle in parts of present-day Ohio and Indiana. U.S. Army and militia forces fare badly against the Indians until Revolutionary War general "Mad Anthony" Wayne forms, trains, and leads a force against the chiefs and their followers at the Battle of Fallen Timbers on August 20, 1794. Wayne's victory is total and opens the Ohio country to settlement.

1787

JULY 13 — Congress passes the Northwest Ordinance, creating the Northwest Territory, bounded by the Great Lakes on the north, the Ohio River on the south, and the Mississippi River on the west. The ordinance organizes this territory, outlines the procedure by which each territory may become a state, and bans slavery from the territory. It is the first federal antislavery legislation.

1787–1788

OCTOBER 1787 – April 1788 — The transition from the Articles of Confederation, which give the states much power and the federal government little, to the Constitution, which gives the federal government great power, proves difficult. To win support for ratification of the Constitution, Alexander Hamilton, James Madison, and John Jay publish a series of essays in New York newspapers between October 1787 and April 1788. Later collected in book form as *The Federalist Papers,* the essays eloquently express the political philosophy of a republican form of government.

1788

JUNE 21 — Thanks in no small measure to the persuasive power of *The Federalist Papers,* the new United States Constitution is ratified. Ratification requires the assent of nine states, and New Hampshire is the ninth to vote for it. The Constitution goes into effect on March 4, 1789, replacing the Articles of Confederation.

1789

THOSE WHO strongly support the Constitution unite to form the Federalist Party, the nation's first political party.

WILLIAM HILL Brown writes and publishes what literary historians consider the first American novel, *The Power of Sympathy; or, The Triumph of Nature,* a tepid moralistic tale intended to "expose the dangerous Consequences of Seduction" and to promote "the advantages of female Education."

1789

MARCH 4 — The First Congress convenes under the new Constitution. George Washington, the first president of the United States, is inaugurated on April 30.

SEPTEMBER 2 — President Washington creates the U.S. Department of the Treasury, bringing the management of the young republic's finances under the close supervision of the president.

SEPTEMBER 26 — John Jay, Washington's appointee as the first chief justice of the U.S. Supreme Court, is confirmed by the Senate.

1790

THE FIRST U.S. census gives the nation's population as 3,929,625, including 697,624 slaves.

MAY 31 — George Washington signs the first U.S. copyright act. Two months later, on July 31, the U.S. Patent Office opens.

1791

DECEMBER 12 — The Bank of the United States opens its main branch in the nation's capital, Philadelphia. The bank is the federal government's designated fiscal representative.

DECEMBER 15 — Virginia becomes the ninth state to ratify the first ten amendments to the Constitution, thereby making the Bill of Rights—an enumeration of personal rights in the United States—the law of the land.

1792

THE FARMER'S ALMANAC is first published and goes on to become a much relied-upon American institution, offering miscellaneous knowledge, practical advice, and a wealth of folklore.

THOMAS JEFFERSON founds the Democratic-Republican Party, which favors the supremacy of the rights of the individual, in opposition to the Federalist Party, which favors the authority of a strong central government.

DECEMBER 5 — George Washington is elected to a second term as president, with 132 electoral votes. John Adams, with 77 electoral votes, is reelected as vice president. An anti-Federalist candidate, George Clinton of New York, garners 50 electoral votes.

1793

FEBRUARY 12 — The Second Congress passes "An act respecting fugitives from justice, and persons escaping from the service of their masters," which authorizes the arrest or seizure of fugitive slaves and provides for a fine of $500 against any person who aids a fugitive slave.

U.S. POPULATION: 3,929,625

APRIL 8 — Edmond Charles Genêt (addressed according to French revolutionary etiquette as Citizen Genêt), a minister to the United States dispatched by the revolutionary French Girondist regime, arrives in Charleston. He begins commissioning privateers (state-sponsored pirates) to sail from American ports to attack British commercial vessels. Deeming this a violation of U.S. sovereignty, President Washington ultimately demands that the French government recall Genêt. By this time, however, the Girondists have been overthrown by the more radical Jacobins, who order Genêt's arrest. Unwilling to send the errant diplomat to the guillotine, Washington refuses extradition. Genêt later becomes a U.S. citizen and marries the daughter of New York governor George Clinton, putting a happy ending to the "Citizen Genêt Affair."

OCTOBER 28 — Yale University graduate Eli Whitney, working as a tutor at Mulberry Grove, a Georgia plantation, applies for a patent on the cotton gin. The device greatly accelerates the removal of seeds from short-staple cotton, making cotton cultivation extremely efficient and profitable. This has two effects: it makes cotton king in the South, and it substantially increases the demand for slave labor to pick cotton, thereby ensuring the continuation of slavery as a Southern institution.

1794

JULY–NOVEMBER — Farmers in western Pennsylvania respond to a federal tax on whiskey (an important source of income for the farmers) by staging the Whiskey Rebellion, in which they menace federal revenue agents and anyone else who tries to enforce the new tax. In an exercise of newfound federal authority under the Constitution, President Washington issues a proclamation on September 24 ordering the militia to suppress the uprising. Two ringleaders are convicted of treason, although they are subsequently pardoned by the president.

NOVEMBER 19 — U.S. treaty negotiator John Jay concludes the so-called Jay Treaty with Great Britain in an effort to improve deteriorating Anglo-American relations. The treaty allows the British to board and search U.S. vessels and to "impress" into the Royal Navy any seamen deemed to be British subjects. Many Americans consider this an affront to U.S. sovereignty, though, and the treaty is widely denounced. Impressment eventually figures as a cause of the War of 1812.

1795

THE GEORGIA legislature grants to four companies 35 million acres of the "Yazoo lands" in present-day Mississippi and Alabama in return for $500,000. It is then discovered that all but one of the Georgia legislators has a financial interest in the grants. A new legislature repeals the sales contracts, but all courts, including the U.S. Supreme Court, uphold the grants. Ultimately, the U.S. Congress votes $4.3 million to settle the claims in the great "Yazoo Land Fraud"—the most spectacular swindle in the history of the early republic.

1796

DECEMBER 7 — John Adams is elected the second president of the United States. Under the law at the time, runner-up Thomas Jefferson becomes vice president, but the two, allies during the American Revolution, become bitter ideological opponents—Adams the standard bearer of the Federalists, Jefferson of the Democratic-Republicans.

1798

APRIL 3 — Seeking to patch up deteriorating Franco-American relations, President John Adams sends a commission to France to negotiate a new treaty of commerce. The commission is met by three French ministers, subsequently referred to in congressional documents as "X, Y, and Z," who inform the commissioners that the United States must loan France $12 million and pay Prime Minister Talleyrand a personal bribe of $250,000 before the treaty can even be discussed. Adams presents the particulars of this diplomatic outrage to Congress on April 3, and the "XYZ Affair" soon becomes public, leading to the Franco-American "Quasi War" and passage of the repressive Alien and Sedition Acts.

JUNE–JULY — A Federalist-dominated Congress passes the Alien and Sedition Acts, consisting of the Naturalization Act (June 18), which raises the residency requirement for naturalization from 5 to 14 years, thereby disqualifying many recently immigrated Democratic-Republicans from voting or running for office; the Alien Act (June 25), authorizing the president to summarily deport aliens he regards as dangerous; the Alien Enemies Act (July 6), authorizing the imprisonment of citizens of hostile countries during times of war; and the Sedition Act (July 14), prohibiting assembly "with intent to oppose any measure of the government" and forbidding the publication of anything "false, scandalous, and malicious" against the government. Essentially counterrevolutionary, the Alien and Sedition Acts are opposed by Thomas Jefferson, James Madison, and other Democratic-Republicans. Jefferson sponsors the repeal of the Sedition Act immediately on taking office as president in 1801, and the other acts quickly expire, except for the Alien Enemies Act, which remains in force.

1798–1800

FRANCE AND the United States fight an undeclared naval war (the Franco-American "Quasi War") because French warships interfere with U.S. merchant ships carrying goods to and from Britain. The fledgling U.S. Navy, including such heroic officers as Stephen Decatur, triumphs. The war is ended with restored Franco-American amity by the Convention between the French Republic and the United States signed on September 30, 1800.

1800

APRIL 24 — The Library of Congress is established.

NOVEMBER 17 — Congress convenes for the first time in Washington, District of Columbia, the new U.S. capital.

1801

FEBRUARY 17 — The election of Thomas Jefferson is decided in the House of Representatives. In the November 1800 election, Jefferson defeated John Adams but was tied with Aaron Burr in the Electoral College, an outcome that sent the contest to the House. Jefferson is finally elected on the 36th ballot, just two weeks before Inauguration Day.

1801–1805

WHEN THE United States abruptly discontinues the practice of paying extortionary tribute to the Barbary States (the Berber countries of North Africa) as protection against state-sponsored piracy, Tripoli declares war on the United States. In the resulting Tripolitan War, the U.S. Navy prevails against the pirates and successfully upholds American sovereignty and its right of international navigation and commerce.

1803

FEBRUARY 24 — In his decision in the case of *Marbury* v. *Madison,* Chief Justice John Marshall finds unconstitutional the law under which Marbury and three others sued Thomas Jefferson's Secretary of State James Madison for failing to deliver commissions (political appointments) granted them during the administration of President John Adams. This decision establishes the Supreme Court's powerful role of "judicial review," the authority to determine the constitutionality

U.S. POPULATION: 5,309,000

of legislation and to declare null and void any law it finds unconstitutional.

APRIL 30 — Thomas Jefferson makes the Louisiana Purchase from France, adding to the United States 828,000 square miles of territory between the Mississippi River and the Rocky Mountains for the price of 80,000,000 francs ($15,000,000).

1804

FEBRUARY 16 — In the Tripolitan War, Stephen Decatur becomes a national hero for the daring exploit of depriving the Tripolitan navy of the captured frigate USS *Philadelphia* when, under the guns of the enemy, he dashes into the harbor at Tripoli, capital of modern Libya, and burns the ship.

MAY 14 — Meriwether Lewis and William Clark leave St. Louis, Missouri, to explore the vast Louisiana Territory and the West beyond the Rocky Mountains. The intrepid Lewis and Clark Expedition is of great scientific value. It reaches the Pacific on November 8, 1805, and returns to St. Louis on September 23, 1806.

JULY 11 — Aaron Burr kills his political archrival Alexander Hamilton in a pistol duel at Weehawken, New Jersey.

DECEMBER 5 — Thomas Jefferson is reelected president, soundly defeating South Carolina Federalist opponent Charles Cotesworth Pinckney.

1805

SACAJAWEA, A Shoshone woman and wife of Toussaint Charbonneau, the official interpreter attached to the Lewis and Clark Expedition, is instrumental in guiding the explorers from what is now South Dakota all the way to the Pacific.

1807

THE COLORFUL fur trader and entrepreneur Manuel Lisa establishes Fort Manuel on the Little Bighorn River, thereby opening the vast Louisiana Territory to the fur trade and inaugurating the era of the far western trappers known as "mountain men," the earliest avant-garde of America's western migration.

AUGUST 7 — Robert Fulton launches the first commercially practical steamboat and steams from New York City to Albany in 32 hours. A year later, Fulton launches and operates the *North River Steamboat of Clermont* (more familiarly shortened to *Clermont*) and becomes a prosperous operator of Hudson River steam transportation.

SEPTEMBER 1 — Aaron Burr, one of the early republic's most controversial political figures, is acquitted of treason in a scheme to annex Spanish territory, gain control of part of the Louisiana Territory, and set up a new empire over which he would reign. Acting in accordance with a strict evidentiary ruling by Supreme Court chief justice John Marshall, who presides over the trial, a jury acquits Burr on the grounds that no evidence of an actual, overt act of treason has been presented and Burr cannot be convicted merely for his unrealized intentions.

DECEMBER 22 — President Jefferson signs the Embargo Act, an economic measure meant to retaliate against Britain and France, which, in their ongoing wars with one another, have repeatedly violated U.S. neutrality rights by interfering with navigation. The act closes U.S. ports to all export shipping, whether in American or foreign vessels, and places restrictions on imports from Great Britain. The embargo quickly does more harm than good to the struggling economy of the youthful United States.

1808

JANUARY 1 — In accordance with a constitutional provision, a U.S. ban on the African slave trade goes into effect.

DECEMBER 7 — Jefferson's protégé and fellow Democratic-Republican James Madison is elected president, defeating the Federalist opponent Charles Pinckney.

1809

MARCH 1 — The Embargo Act of 1808 is replaced by the less restrictive Non-Intercourse Act. The new act reopens U.S. ports to ships of all nations except France and England and outlaws imports from either country. Even this milder version of the embargo proves economically ruinous.

1811

NOVEMBER 7 — Gen. William Henry Harrison defeats the Shawnee Indian leader Tecumseh at Tippecanoe, Indiana. This is the beginning of the end of Tecumseh's efforts to unite the Indians of the Old Northwest in resistance to white settlement of their lands.

DECEMBER 16 — The New Madrid (Missouri) earthquake hits. Perhaps the strongest earthquake in recorded history, it alters the topography of some 30,000 square miles, changes the course of the Mississippi River, and even causes the river to flow backwards for a time, creating Redfoot Lake in Tennessee. The human toll is not well documented but certainly slight because the region is very thinly populated.

1812–1814

THE WAR OF 1812 (with Britain) and the related Creek War (against the Red Stick faction of the Creek Indian tribe) are fought. So-called War Hawks in Congress promote the War of 1812 as a means of acquiring additional territory for the United States but it proves nearly disastrous.

1812

MARCH 3 — Congress passes the first foreign aid bill, voting relief in the amount of $50,000 for victims of an earthquake in Venezuela.

MAY 14 — Congress annexes the former Spanish territory of West Florida, adding it to the Mississippi territory and the nation.

AUGUST 15 — In the War of 1812, British-allied Potawatomi Indians attack Fort Dearborn, at the site of present-day Chicago. A war party led by Chief Blackbird ambushes 96 soldiers and civilians as they evacuate, killing about 50.

AUGUST 16 — In one of the great American humiliations of the War of 1812, Brig. Gen. William Hull, the superannuated commander of U.S. militia forces assigned to invade British Canada, falls back under attack and surrenders Detroit to the British without firing a shot.

1812

DECEMBER 2 — James Madison is reelected president, defeating DeWitt Clinton, a candidate endorsed by the Federalists as well as by members of Madison's own Democratic-Republican Party who are opposed to the ongoing War of 1812.

DURING THE War of 1812, the U.S. Navy consistently outperforms American ground forces. In spectacular one-on-one combat, USS *Constitution* ("Old Ironsides") defeats HMS *Guerrière* (August 19) and *Java* (December 29).

1813

SEPTEMBER 10 — Oliver Hazard Perry, having cobbled together an inland U.S. fleet, defeats a Royal Navy flotilla in the Battle of Lake Erie. This victory cuts off the British army's waterborne supply route and facilitates Gen.

U.S. POPULATION: 7,239,000

William Henry Harrison's victory at the Battle of the Thames (in Ontario, Canada). Perry sends a memorable dispatch to Harrison: "We have met the enemy, and they are ours."

OCTOBER 5 — William Henry Harrison defeats combined British and Indian forces in Ontario, Canada at the Battle of the Thames. The great Indian war leader Tecumseh is slain; with him dies the last hope of a confederacy among the Indian tribes of the Old Northwest.

1814

MARCH 27 — Gen. Andrew Jackson defeats the Red Stick Creek Indians at the Battle of Horseshoe Bend, Alabama, ending the Creek War. By the Treaty of Horseshoe Bend, the Creek yield almost all of their tribal lands to the United States.

AUGUST 24 — British general Robert Ross invades Washington, D.C., putting to the torch most government buildings, including the Capitol and White House.

SEPTEMBER 13–14 — Detained by the British aboard a warship in Baltimore Harbor, lawyer Francis Scott Key anxiously passes the night by observing the British naval bombardment of Fort McHenry, which guards the approach to Baltimore. When the dawn's early light reveals that the star-spangled American banner yet waves, signifying that the British have failed to capture the fort, Key pens the verses that—later set to an old English tavern tune ("To

Anacreon in Heaven")—are the words to what most Americans come to consider the country's national anthem. By executive order, President Herbert Hoover makes "The Star-Spangled Banner" the official national anthem in 1931.

DECEMBER 15, 1814 – JANUARY 5, 1815 — The five New England states, heavily Federalist in political allegiance and bitterly opposed to the War of 1812 from the beginning, convene at the Hartford (Connecticut) Convention to debate secession from the United States. The signing of the Treaty of Ghent (Belgium), however, ends the war, and also ends the convention by making secession unnecessary. But the fact of the convention taints the Federalists as disloyal, dealing a crippling blow to this moribund party.

DECEMBER 24 — U.S. and British negotiators conclude the Treaty of Ghent, ending the War of 1812 by reestablishing the *status quo ante bellum* ("the state of things before the war"). Neither side officially gains anything from the terms of the treaty, but despite suffering more military defeats than victories, the United States emerges from the war having successfully defended its sovereignty against encroachment by the greatest military and naval power in the world. For this reason, some historians call the War of 1812 America's "second war of independence."

1815

JANUARY 8 — Gen. Andrew Jackson brilliantly leads a mixed force of U.S. Army regulars, militiamen, volunteers, and even the celebrated pirate Jean Lafitte—about 4,500 men in all—against 7,500 British veterans of the Napoleonic Wars under Sir Edward Pakenham at the Battle of New Orleans. Word of the war-ending Treaty of Ghent had failed to reach either the British invaders of New Orleans or the defenders of the city under Jackson. In the course of a half-hour battle, the British are repulsed, having suffered 2,036 dead or wounded, with Pakenham among the slain. The Battle of New Orleans leaves many Americans with the unfounded sense that the War of 1812 has been a great American triumph and the well-founded impression that Andrew Jackson is a military hero.

MARCH 3 — The Algerine War—war against Algiers—is declared by Congress in response to state-sanctioned piracy against American ships. As with the earlier Tripolitan War, the United States refuses to pay protection money in the form of tribute. The war is quickly won.

1816

DECEMBER 4 — James Monroe, a Democratic-Republican, is elected president, easily defeating New York's Rufus King, the Federalist candidate.

1817

MARCH 3 — Outgoing president James Madison vetoes the "Bonus Bill" on his last day in office. The bill would have provided federal funds for "internal improvements" such as roads and canals. Madison favors such projects, but he believes that a constitutional amendment is necessary to allow the federal government to pay for them.

July 4 — In the absence of federal funding, New York raises its own funds to begin construction of the Erie Canal. Connecting New York City with the Great Lakes via the Hudson River, the canal is completed on October 25, 1825, and opens the frontier to trade with the East Coast. It is a tremendous financial and economic success.

September — Written when he was only 18, William Cullen Bryant publishes "Thantatopsis," the first American poem to capture an international audience.

1817–1818

The First Seminole War begins on November 20, 1817, when settlers attack the Seminole, who retaliate by raiding homesteads in northern Florida and southern Georgia. The United States pushes for widespread annexation of Seminole lands. The war ends inconclusively because of exhaustion on both sides.

1819

Washington Irving's *Sketch Book* (which includes such stories as "The Legend of Sleepy Hollow" and "Rip Van Winkle") is published. Irving becomes the first internationally acclaimed American fiction writer.

A combination of heavy government debt incurred during the War of 1812, high protective tariffs, wild speculation in western lands, overextended industrial capital invest-ment, and the shrinkage of foreign markets for American goods bring on bank failures and the rapid devaluation of paper currency. The result is the Panic of 1819, one of the worst short-term financial crises in American history.

FEBRUARY — In *McCulloch* v. *Maryland,* the U.S. Supreme Court (Chief Justice John Marshall presiding) rules that the Second Bank of the United States is constitutional and, in the process, provides a broad constitutional man-date for Congress, holding that the legislative branch has the power to make "all laws…necessary and proper" to execute the powers enumerated for it by the Constitution.

FEBRUARY 13 — Representative James Tallmadge of New York introduces an antislavery amendment to the Missouri Statehood Bill. Under constitutional challenge, the amendment is dropped.

MARCH 2 — Congress enacts the first immigration law, establishing standard procedures for passenger ships transporting immigrants and mandating the compila-tion of accurate statistics on immigration.

1820

MARCH 3 — Congress passes the Missouri Compromise, engineered by Kentucky's Henry Clay to maintain the precarious balance between the congressional repre-sentation of slave states and free states. Maine is admitted as a free state and Missouri as a slave state, thereby keeping representation equal—but slavery is barred in the rest of the Louisiana Purchase north of latitude 36° 30'.

DECEMBER 6 — James Monroe is reelected president, defeating diehard Federalist John Quincy Adams 231 electoral votes to 1.

1821

DECEMBER — Stephen Austin founds the first American colony, San Felipe de Austin, in Texas, at that time part of Mexico.

1822

THE FIRST African-American emigrants depart for Liberia, a colony established in western Africa in 1821 by the American Colonization Society, a philanthropic organization founded to advance an emerging American back-to-Africa movement. By the time the emigration ends after the Civil War, about 15,000 African Americans will have settled in Liberia.

1823

DECEMBER 2 — President James Monroe promulgates the "Monroe Doctrine" in his annual message to Congress. The doctrine puts Europe on notice that the United States will resist any attempt to establish colonies in the Western Hemisphere or otherwise to interfere in the affairs of the region. The doctrine further states the intention of the United States to hold itself aloof from European affairs.

1824

SEQUOYAH, THE son of a white trader and a Cherokee woman, creates the first written Indian alphabet and language, committing the Cherokee tongue to writing.

1825

JANUARY 3 — Social reformer Robert Owen founds a utopian community at New Harmony, Indiana. Run on principles of total equality, it is peopled by about 1,000 highly educated idealists, who soon fall to bickering. Owen leaves in 1827, and the utopian experiment ends the following year.

FEBRUARY 9 — The House of Representatives elects John Quincy Adams president over Andrew Jackson. Neither candidate had received an electoral majority in the December 1, 1824, presidential election, so the contest was sent to the House of Representatives, as required by the Constitution.

1827

JAMES FENIMORE COOPER publishes *The Prairie*, featuring Natty Bumppo (also known as Hawkeye, Deerslayer, and Leather-stocking), an archetypal frontiersman. Together with the other novels of the "Leatherstocking Tales" (including *The Deerslayer, Last of the Mohicans, The Pathfinder*, and *The Pioneers), The Prairie* tells the epic story of America's expansion into the wilderness. All of the books become international bestsellers.

U.S. POPULATION: 9,638,453

1828

THE DEMOCRATIC PARTY is formed. Essentially an out-growth of Thomas Jefferson's Democratic-Republican Party, the new party consists of the Northern urban working class and Southern agrarians. The new party promotes broader enfranchisement, favors a loosening of tight credit, and generally extols the "common man." Andrew Jackson is its first presidential nominee.

JULY 4 — Ground is broken for the nation's first commercial railroad, the Baltimore and Ohio.

DECEMBER — Henry Clay pushes through Congress a high protective tariff to foster American industry. The Southern states, whose export trade in cotton suffers as a result, condemns this as the "Tariff of Abominations" (a phrase first used in the South Carolina legislature on December 19), and the first rumblings of "states' rights" and secession are heard.

DECEMBER 3 — Andrew Jackson, identified as the champion of the "common man," is elected president, defeating incumbent John Quincy Adams. His election ushers in the "Age of Jackson," a period in which democracy is further liberalized and westward expansion is aggressively promoted—typically at the expense of the Indians.

1830

JANUARY 19–27 — The Webster-Hayne debates take place in the Senate. Robert Y. Hayne of South Carolina defends the doctrine of states' rights, whereas Daniel Webster holds that the individual states are sovereign only where their power is not limited by the Constitution, and he further argues that the Constitution and the federal government are sovereign not over the states but over the people of the United States. The debates establish the framework of the opposing ideologies of government in which the Civil War will develop.

APRIL 6 — At Fayette, New York, Joseph Smith founds the Mormon Church with 30 members. Its theology is based on *The Book of Mormon,* a scripture Smith published in 1829 as his translation of golden tablets he claims to have unearthed in 1827 at Palmyra, New York.

MAY 28 — President Jackson signs the Indian Removal Act. It calls for the "removal" of all Indians living east of the Mississippi River and their resettlement in Indian Territory (encompassing present-day Oklahoma and parts of some adjacent states).

1831

THE NAME "Underground Railroad" is first used to describe the loose network of white abolitionists, free blacks, and former slaves dedicated to helping fugitive slaves escape from the South to freedom in the Northern states.

JANUARY 1 — William Lloyd Garrison of Boston publishes the first issue of *The Liberator,* which galvanizes the abolitionist cause and denies any possibility of compromise with those who favor slavery.

AUGUST 22 — Just before dawn, Nat Turner, a slave and lay preacher, leads 50 or more fellow slaves in a rebellion in Southampton County, Virginia. Sixty whites are killed in the uprising before Turner and most of his band are caught. Turner and 19 followers are quickly tried and hanged, and local whites retaliate against the uprising by randomly killing African Americans in the area.

1832

April 6 — The Black Hawk War begins when the Sac and Fox chief Black Hawk and his followers (known as the British Band, because of their allegiance to the British during the War of 1812) clash with Illinois settlers on land they relinquished under a fraudulent treaty. After raiding and counterraiding, the war ends at the mouth of the Bad Axe River in Wisconsin, where many of the British Band are massacred by Illinois militia under Gen. Henry Atkinson.

NOVEMBER 24 — In response to the "Tariff of Abominations," a convention called by the South Carolina legislature passes the Ordinance of Nullification, asserting that the tariff is unconstitutional and therefore null and void. The doctrine of nullification holds that a state may nullify any federal law it deems unconstitutional. President Jackson responds

U.S. POPULATION: 12,866,000

by threatening military action, and the nation seems on the verge of civil war; however, the Nullification Crisis is resolved by a compromise tariff, passed in March 1833.

DECEMBER 5 — Andrew Jackson is reelected president by a wide majority over Henry Clay.

1832–1836

PRESIDENT JACKSON goes to war against the Second Bank of the United States, which he and his supporters see as exerting a stranglehold on the credit needed by western entrepreneurs seeking to advance the frontiers of settlement and enterprise. Jackson vetoes the bill that would have renewed the bank's charter and issues an executive order withdrawing all federal funds from it. By 1836, the bank closes its doors, freeing up credit and helping the West to expand, but also introducing a high degree of volatility into the American economy, thereby creating a wild era of boom and bust.

1833

ACCORDING TO some sports historians, baseball is "invented" by the Olympic Ball Club in Philadelphia. A development of various children's games, the Olympic's version resembles English cricket more than it does modern baseball, the rules of which will not be formalized for another dozen years.

1834

CYRUS MCCORMICK patents a new horse-drawn mechanical reaper, which revolutionizes agriculture, accomplishing in a single hour what takes 20 hours by hand labor.

DAVY CROCKETT publishes his autobiography, *Narrative of the Life of David Crockett,* which contributes to his legendary renown as a Tennessee frontiersman turned congressman. The book becomes the basis for many subsequent works of fiction, including dime novels and melodramas as well as (in the 20th century) movies and television shows.

JUNE 30 — The Department of Indian Affairs is established by act of Congress in an attempt to formulate and enforce a uniform federal policy toward Native Americans.

1835–1836

THE TEXAS WAR OF INDEPENDENCE is fought to transform Texas from a Mexican territory colonized by American nationals to a sovereign republic, with an eye toward eventual annexation to the United States.

1835–1842

THE SECOND SEMINOLE WAR is fought in Florida and Georgia against the Seminole and closely allied Creek who resist their "removal" to the West as required by the Indian Removal Act of 1830. The war sees the rise of a charismatic and skillful war chief, Osceola, and ends inconclusively in 1842 when the U.S. government stops trying to locate and remove those Seminole who remain in Florida and Georgia. For every two Seminole apprehended and sent west, one U.S. Army soldier is killed in battle: 1,500 in all. The war costs the Treasury $20 million.

1836

WILLIAM MCGUFFEY, a professor at Miami University of Ohio, publishes the first of his famous *McGuffey Readers* for the instruction of elementary schoolchildren. The *Readers* go on to influence generations of Americans, teaching them not only how to read but also providing them instruction in religion, morality, ethics, and patriotism.

BLACKSMITH JOHN DEERE of Grand Detour, Illinois, produces his first steel plow, the "Grand Detour Plow," which is specially designed to break the tough, root-bound soil of the Western prairies. The new plow makes prairie farming practical and thereby facilitates the settlement of the Great Plains.

FEBRUARY 25 — Samuel Colt patents the revolver. His weapons become icons of both law and lawlessness in the American West.

MARCH 2 — Texas declares its independence from Mexico. A garrison of 187 Texans, led by William B. Travis and including the legendary frontiersmen Jim Bowie and Davy Crockett, defends the Alamo, a San Antonio mission turned fortress, against a vastly superior force commanded by Gen. Antonio López de Santa Anna. After a siege, the Alamo falls on March 6, and the garrison is slaughtered, thereby providing the cause of Texas independence with heroic martyrs and a powerful battle cry: "Remember the Alamo!"

APRIL 21 — Led by the brave and highly skilled Sam Houston, an army of Texans meets the forces of Santa Anna at the Battle of San Jacinto. After a fierce 15-minute exchange, the Mexican forces are routed and many Mexican troops are slaughtered in retribution for the massacre at the Alamo. Santa Anna disguises himself in an effort to elude capture, but he is found and, under pain of death, signs the Treaty of Velasco, by which the Mexican government recognizes the independence of Texas.

SEPTEMBER 1 — Two missionaries, Dr. Marcus Whitman and H. H. Spaulding, together with their families, establish the first American settlement in the Oregon Territory. This toehold soon gives way to a rush of Far Western settlement dubbed "Oregon fever."

DECEMBER 7 — Martin Van Buren, handpicked by Andrew Jackson as his successor, is elected president.

1837

AUGUST 31 — Ralph Waldo Emerson delivers a speech titled "The American Scholar" before the Phi Beta Kappa Society at Harvard University. Intended to awaken Americans to the value and vitality of their own artistic, literary, and philosophical culture—which, he urges, need not slavishly copy the cultures of the Old World—the speech is hailed as "our intellectual Declaration of Independence" by Oliver Wendell Holmes, Sr.

1838

DECEMBER — Thousands of Cherokee begin the "Trail of Tears" march to forced resettlement in Indian Territory (present-day Oklahoma and parts of some adjacent states). Of 15,000 who make the 1,200-mile journey from the Southeast, 4,000 die en route in what one U.S. Army soldier assigned to escort duty calls "the cruelest work I ever knew."

1840

EDGAR ALLAN POE publishes *Tales of the Grotesque and Arabesque*, an innovative early collection of short fiction.

DECEMBER 2 — William Henry ("Tippecanoe") Harrison is elected president (and John Tyler vice president) after conducting the first "modern" presidential campaign, complete with catchy slogan—"Tippecanoe and Tyler, too!"—and arresting icon: the log cabin, symbol of Harrison's frontier lineage and affiliation.

1841

VOLNEY PALMER of Philadelphia becomes the nation's first ad agent and coins the term "advertising agency," thereby inaugurating a powerfully influential American industry.

APRIL 1 — Members of the Transcendental Club, a group of New England intellectuals and idealists, form the Brook Farm Association. Led by George Ripley, approximately 20 members begin a utopian experiment, living on Brook Farm and balancing simple manual labor with exalted intellectual pursuits. The Brook Farm experiment ends in 1847.

APRIL 4 — Having contracted pneumonia after delivering an excessively long inauguration speech in frigid Washington weather, William Henry Harrison dies just one month after taking office. He is succeeded by Vice President John Tyler.

MAY — The first covered wagon train departs for California. The covered wagon will come to symbolize the Western pioneer experience.

1841–1842

DOROTHEA DIX conducts a two-year investigation into the treatment of the insane in Massachusetts. Her findings become the basis of a humanitarian reform campaign that influences legislation in 11 states.

1842

THOMAS W. DORR leads "Dorr's Rebellion" in Rhode Island after the legislature fails to reform the state constitution, essentially unchanged since Rhode Island was established as a colony in 1663. Dorr's followers draft a new constitution and elect Dorr governor. Samuel W. King, the legitimately elected governor, declares martial law, and Dorr, with others, is arrested on May 18 when his attempt to seize the state armory fails. Sentenced to life imprisonment in 1843, Dorr is pardoned after one year, and the reforms he and his followers had sought—

principally "universal manhood suffrage," that is, the right to vote without a property ownership requirement—are adopted.

MARCH 3 — Massachusetts governor John Davis signs the nation's first law regulating child labor, mandating no more than a ten-hour workday for children under age 12.

1843

POPULAR FIDDLER Dan Emmett debuts his Virginia Minstrels, white entertainers in blackface, who present a "plantation-style" song-and-dance show to audiences in New York City's Bowery Amphitheatre. Called a "minstrel show," it features a comic, sanitized, and idealized image of slave plantation life, and goes on to become an enduring staple of American popular culture. It is the nation's first commercial mass entertainment.

MAY 22 — The "Great Migration" to Oregon begins as the first 1,000 settlers depart from Independence, Missouri. Drawn to the settlement Dr. Marcus Whitman and H. H. Spaulding have established in Oregon, the Great Migration passes along the Oregon Trail, stretching from Independence to Oregon's Willamette Valley.

1844

MAY 24 — American painter and inventor Samuel F. B. Morse sends the first message on the telegraph he has

U.S. POPULATION: 17,069,453

invented. The question "What hath God wrought?" is transmitted over some 40 miles of wire from the main chamber of the U.S. Supreme Court in Washington to Alfred Vail in Baltimore.

DECEMBER 4 — Campaigning on the slogan "Fifty-four forty or fight," James K. Polk wins election as president. The slogan refers to the ongoing dispute with Britain over the boundary between Oregon and Canada. Polk and his supporters demand that the boundary be fixed at latitude 54° 40' north, a large territorial gain for the United States.

1845

FREDERICK DOUGLASS, a brilliant self-educated former slave famed as an abolitionist activist and lecturer, publishes his autobiography, *Narrative of the Life of Frederick Douglass,* a bestseller that conveys the profound humanity of the slaves even as it delineates the gross inhumanity of the institution of slavery.

THE MANHATTAN-BASED Knickerbocker Base Ball Club formalizes and writes down the rules of baseball, a sport many believe originated in Philadelphia in 1833.

JULY — Discussing the annexation of Texas, *New York Post* editor John L. O'Sullivan writes in the *United States Magazine and Democratic Review,* "It is our manifest destiny to overspread and possess the whole of the continent which Providence has given us for the development of the great experiment of liberty and federated self-government entrusted to us." The phrase "manifest destiny" instantly becomes a justification for United States' possession of territory from the Atlantic to the Pacific, even if acquiring the land means war.

DECEMBER 29 — After nearly a decade as an independent republic, Texas is admitted to the Union, thereby virtually ensuring a war with Mexico.

1846

MAY 1 — The Mexican War begins on the Texas border. The United States formally declares war on May 13. The conflict ends, in a resounding U.S. victory, on February 2, 1848.

JUNE 14 — A small band of Americans living in Alta California, a Mexican territory, declares independence from Mexico in the Bear Flag Revolt (named after the flag of the rebels, which features a California brown bear—the symbol on the current state flag of California). The revolt quickly merges into the more general Mexican War that began along the Texas-Mexico border.

1847

MARCH 22 — During the Mexican War, Maj. Gen. Winfield Scott leads the American army in its first-ever amphibious operation: a landing at Veracruz. From here, Scott conducts a brilliant march on Mexico City.

MAY 1 — The Smithsonian Institution is formally dedicated in Washington, D.C., having been funded by the bequest of British scientist James Smithson "for the increase and diffusion of knowledge among men" and chartered by act of Congress in 1846.

JULY 24 — Led by Brigham Young, 148 Mormons—143 men, 3 women, and 2 children—arrive in Salt Lake City, Utah Territory. They are the vanguard of the great Mormon Trek, the mass migration of a millennial religious group seeking to establish a new Zion in the American West, remote from the persecution that has afflicted it since Joseph Smith (murdered by anti-Mormon vigilantes on June 27, 1844) founded it in 1830 at Fayette, New York.

SEPTEMBER 14 — In the culminating battle of the Mexican War, Maj. Gen. Winfield Scott enters Mexico City.

1848

IN A major breakthrough for women's rights, New York State passes the Married Women's Property Act of 1848, granting women property rights equal to those of men.

JANUARY 24 — James Marshall, an employee of John A. Sutter, discovers gold in the race of a mill on Sutter's ranch. Within a year, the California Gold Rush begins, drawing thousands of "forty-niners" (prospectors who arrive in 1849), instantly populating the territory, and making California statehood an urgent issue.

FEBRUARY 2 — The Treaty of Guadalupe Hidalgo ends the Mexican War. In return for the cession to the United

States of "New Mexico" (encompassing the present state of New Mexico and portions of the present states of Utah, Nevada, Arizona, and Colorado) and California, as well as the renunciation of claims to Texas above the Rio Grande, the United States pays Mexico $15,000,000 and assumes all claims of U.S. citizens against Mexico, which (as later determined by a specially appointed commission) amount to an additional $3,250,000.

JUNE 3 — The first treaty between the United States and New Grenada (modern Colombia) for rights to build the Panama Canal is signed, but nothing comes of the project for more than 50 years.

JULY 19–20 — Suffragists Lucretia Mott and Elizabeth Cady Stanton convene a women's conference at Seneca Falls, New York, to discuss and debate voting rights and property rights for women.

NOVEMBER 7 — Zachary Taylor, hero of the Mexican War, is elected president, defeating Democrat Lewis Cass.

1849

MARCH 3 — Congress creates the U.S. Department of the Interior to administer the General Land Office, the Bureau of Indian Affairs, the Pension Office, the Patent Office, and the Bureau of the Census.

MAY 10 — The Astor Place Riot breaks out in New York City outside the Astor Place Opera House when a mob protests

British actor William Charles Macready's criticism of what he calls the "barbaric vulgarity" of American life and violently voices support of American actor Edwin Forrest, who is perceived as a champion of the common man. Troops are called to quell the riot, in which 22 die and 56 are injured.

1850

NEW ENGLAND novelist and short-story writer Nathaniel Hawthorne publishes his masterpiece, *The Scarlet Letter,* a beautifully wrought story of secret passion, shared humanity, guilt, and redemption set in Puritan New England.

PHILADELPHIA MERCHANTS become the first in the nation to employ female clerks.

MARCH — Congress reaches the Compromise of 1850, by which California is admitted to the Union as a free state and all other territories acquired as a result of the Mexican War are subject to "popular sovereignty" (the people of each territory will be allowed to decide whether to permit or forbid slavery). Like the Missouri Compromise before it, the Compromise of 1850 staves off civil war even as it continues to stir national discontent.

APRIL 19 — The Clayton-Bulwer Treaty between the United States and Great Britain is signed, guaranteeing that the as-yet-unbuilt Panama Canal will be neutral and open to all nations.

JULY 9 — The death of President Zachary Taylor from cholera elevates Millard Fillmore to the presidency.

SEPTEMBER 18 — The strengthened Fugitive Slave Law of the Compromise of 1850 is passed. The legislation replaces the law of 1793 and, under severe penalty, requires the return of escaped slaves to their owners. Fugitive slaves are barred from jury trial and from testifying in their own defense.

SEPTEMBER 20 — As part of the Compromise of 1850, the slave market is closed in Washington, D.C. The closing suggests the shame most lawmakers feel over the issue of slavery.

1851

HERMAN MELVILLE publishes *Moby-Dick,* among the most ambitious, most original, and greatest of all American novels. The book is a commercial failure and does not enter the pantheon of great American literature until its rediscovery by literary scholars in the late 1920s.

AUGUST 22 — The American yacht *America* wins the One Hundred Guinea Cup, defeating 14 British yachts off the southern coast of England in a race around the Isle of Wight organized by the Royal Yacht Squadron. From this day on, the race and trophy are known as the America's Cup.

U.S. POPULATION: 23,191,867

1852

ABOLITIONIST HARRIET BEECHER STOWE publishes *Uncle Tom's Cabin; or, Life Among the Lowly,* a novel depicting the inhumanity and horrors of plantation slavery. Southerners denounce the novel, which becomes a worldwide bestseller of unprecedented proportions: 300,000 copies are sold in 1852 alone. President Abraham Lincoln (among others) later expresses his belief that the book helped trigger the Civil War.

NOVEMBER 2 — Democrat Franklin Pierce defeats Winfield Scott and is elected president. Scott is the last presidential candidate of the original Whig Party, founded in 1834 mainly to oppose what some perceived as the tyranny of Andrew Jackson. It borrows its name from the British political party that opposed arbitrary royal prerogatives.

1853

THE KNOW-NOTHING PARTY, also called the Native American Party, is formed. Members are anti-Catholic, seek to exclude immigrants from political office, and favor the repeal of all naturalization laws. A secret, even subversive society, the name "Know-Nothing" refers to the response members give when asked about the party and its policies.

DECEMBER 30 — James Gadsden, the U.S. minister to Mexico, negotiates the Gadsden Purchase from Mexico. The U.S. adds 29,644 square miles of territory (parts of

Arizona and New Mexico) to land acquired as a result of the Mexican War.

1854

HENRY DAVID THOREAU, a freelance philosopher, publishes *Walden*, his first-person masterpiece about living minimally and meaningfully on the shores of Walden Pond near Concord, Massachusetts.

MARCH 31 — Having boldly entered Uraga Harbor on July 8, 1853, with four warships, Commodore Matthew C. Perry refuses to leave Japan until he negotiates the Treaty of Kanagawa with that country. After months of talk, the Japanese (who understand that their defenses are inadequate to oppose an entire navy of what they call Perry's "black ships") are intimidated into opening trade with the United States and allowing the installation of a U.S. consul in the country.

MAY 30 — President Pierce signs the Kansas-Nebraska Act, creating the territories of Kansas and Nebraska and declaring them subject to "popular sovereignty"—that is, the citizens of each territory, not the federal government, will decide whether to apply for statehood as a free state or a slave state. Nebraska peacefully votes itself free, but Kansas erupts into violence.

JULY 6 — The Republican Party is founded in a convention at Jackson, Michigan. An antislavery party, the Republicans are united in opposition to the Kansas-

Nebraska Act and include former Whigs, northern Democrats, and former members of various "Free Soil" (antislavery) parties. The new party does much to consolidate political opposition to slavery.

DECEMBER 30 — America's first oil corporation, the Pennsylvania Rock Oil Company, is founded. At the time, oil is most widely used for lighting, lubrication, and certain medicines.

1854–1861

KANSAS ENDURES a bloody guerrilla civil war between proslavery and antislavery factions vying for control first of the territory and then of the state.

1855

WALT WHITMAN, a mostly self-taught newspaper editor and schoolteacher, publishes *Leaves of Grass,* perhaps the most original collection of verse ever written. The poems embody the spirit of democratic America and move Ralph Waldo Emerson to write to Whitman, "I greet you at the beginning of a great career." Whitman continues to shape and enlarge *Leaves of Grass* through several editions until the end of his life in 1892.

1856

FREDERICK LAW OLMSTED is hired by the city of New York to plan and supervise the creation of Central Park, transforming 843 acres of Manhattan, blighted with squatters' shanties, into one of the world's loveliest and most celebrated urban green spaces.

MAY 22 — Antislavery Massachusetts senator Charles Sumner is severely beaten with a cane by South Carolina representative Preston S. Brooks in the Senate in retaliation for his having maligned the state of South Carolina and one of its senators, Andrew P. Butler, Brooks's uncle. To the North, the caning represents Southern brutality at its worst. Sumner's injuries are so serious that his recovery takes some three years. Brooks resigns from Congress, but is reelected in 1858.

MAY 24 — Radical abolitionist John Brown raids a proslavery stronghold at Pottawatomie Creek, Kansas, in retaliation for a May 21 attack on the abolitionist town of Lawrence. Brown and his four sons wield sabers to hack to death five proslavery Kansans.

NOVEMBER 4 — Democrat James Buchanan is elected president, defeating Republican John C. Frémont and other candidates, including Millard Fillmore, who runs on both the Whig and Know-Nothing tickets. The election marks the end of the Whig Party—moribund since the defeat of Winfield Scott in 1852—and it brings into the White House the only bachelor to serve in the office. He proves a fatally passive president and does nothing effective to avert the approach of civil war.

1857

MARCH 6 — Chief Justice Roger Taney hands down the Supreme Court's decision in *Dred Scott* v. *Sandford*. Scott, a slave whose owner had taken him from the slave state of Missouri to the free state of Illinois, sued for his freedom in 1846 on the grounds that his sojourn into free territory had made him free. The court rules that neither slaves nor free blacks are citizens and therefore they cannot sue, and it further rules that the Missouri Compromise (under which suit was brought) is unconstitutional because Congress has no authority to prohibit slavery in the territories. The decision also declares the Missouri Compromise to be in violation of the Fifth Amendment because it deprives slave owners of their "property" without due process of law. By affirming constitutional protection of slavery in all circumstances, the *Dred Scott* decision ends the possibility of compromise on the slavery issue. Only a new constitutional amendment can now bring an end to slavery. Thus the outbreak of civil war is virtually assured.

SEPTEMBER 11 — Mormon zealot John D. Lee leads the Mountain Meadows Massacre, killing 120 California-bound emigrants. Lee cites President Buchanan's removal of Brigham Young as governor of Utah as the provocation for this instance of religious extremism.

OCTOBER 19 — A Constitutional Convention meets in Lecompton, the capital of the Kansas Territory, and presents a constitution for popular referendum, the outcome of which is rigged to ensure that Kansas will enter the Union as a slave state. The Lecompton Constitutional Convention splits an already violent Kansas, which votes down the proslavery constitution on January 4, 1858. Guerrilla warfare ravages both territory and state.

1858

GERMAN-BORN American painter Albert Bierstadt joins a Western survey expedition headed by Frederick W. Lander and makes sketches of the spectacular Rocky Mountain landscape. He later transforms these studies into large-scale painted masterpieces that both capture and excite the world's imagination by creating a visual mythology of the American West as a sublime earthly paradise and land of infinite promise.

AUGUST 16–17 — Queen Victoria of Great Britain transmits the first trans-Atlantic cable message to President James Buchanan over lines laid on the floor of the ocean. Transmission commences at 10:50 a.m. on August 16 and is completed at 4:30 a.m. the next day, a total of 17 hours and 40 minutes to send 99 words consisting of 509 letters. *Nearly* instantaneous international communication is born.

OCTOBER 9 — After a 24-day trip, a stagecoach arrives in St. Louis from San Francisco carrying America's first transcontinental overland mail.

1859

AUGUST 27 — William Smith, employed as a drilling expert by pioneer oil entrepreneur Edwin L. Drake, strikes oil near Titusville, Pennsylvania. His 60-foot-deep well is the first to produce oil, yielding 20 barrels a day and transforming a sleepy business (which hitherto had barreled only "rock oil," oil that had spontaneously found its way to the surface) into a titanic American energy business.

SEPTEMBER 5 — *Our Nig,* by Harriet E. Wilson, is published. It is the first novel by an African American.

OCTOBER 4 — Having rejected the fraudulent proslavery Lecompton Constitution, Kansas voters adopt an anti-slavery constitution. Violence continues between proslavery and antislavery factions even after Kansas is admitted to the Union as a free state in 1861.

OCTOBER 16 — Radical abolitionist John Brown, famed (or notorious) for his violent 1856 vengeance against proslavery settlers in "Bleeding Kansas," leads 21 followers in the seizure of the federal arsenal at Harpers Ferry, Virginia (now West Virginia). His objective is to provoke a widespread slave rebellion and to establish an abolitionist republic in the Appalachians, made up of fugitive slaves and white abolitionists. A contingent of U.S. Marines under the temporary command of Robert E. Lee (then an officer in the U.S. Army) quickly retakes the arsenal, and Brown is arrested, tried, and hanged (on December 2) for murder, conspiracy, and treason against Virginia. For even moderate abolitionists, Brown becomes a martyr to the cause of African-American liberty.

1860

OLIVER F. WINCHESTER produces the first commercially viable repeating rifle in his New Haven, Connecticut, arms factory. The rifle soon becomes an icon of the expansion of the American West.

APRIL 3 — The first Pony Express rider leaves St. Joseph, Missouri (eastern terminus of the Express). The final rider in a relay of couriers arrives in Sacramento on April 13. Although it ceases operation in October 1861 (rendered obsolete by the transcontinental telegraph), the Pony Express enters American lore as a great romantic Western enterprise calling on the boundless bravery and endurance of intrepid lone riders.

MAY 10 — The Morrill Tariff Bill is passed by the House of Representatives, ushering in an era of protectionism to foster American industry. Citizens of the industrial North see the bill as a great boon, whereas those of the agricultural South regard it as a disaster, reducing foreign demand for cotton and other agricultural goods. The Morrill Tariff Bill widens the already yawning gulf between North and South.

NOVEMBER 6 — Abraham Lincoln, the candidate of the anti-slavery Republican Party, is elected president, defeating the two candidates of a splintered Democratic Party. The combined vote for his opponents exceeds Lincoln's total, making him president by a plurality rather than a majority. The election of the man Southerners call "Black Lincoln" provokes the secession of the Southern states.

DECEMBER 18 — With civil war rapidly approaching, Kentucky senator John J. Crittenden proposes constitutional amendments to extend the line originally drawn in the now-defunct Missouri Compromise across the entire nation, permitting slavery below the line and prohibiting it above. Lincoln opposes the Crittenden Compromise, a last-ditch attempt to stave off secession and war, and it fails.

DECEMBER 20 — South Carolina, long a hotbed of states' rights advocacy, becomes the first Southern state to secede from the Union.

1860–1868

EVEN AS the Civil War approaches and is fought, mainly in the East, the Apache and Navajo War erupts in the West and continues sporadically for more than eight years.

1861–1865

THE CIVIL WAR begins on April 12, 1861, and ends definitively, with the defeat of the Confederacy, on May 26,

U.S. POPULATION: 31,443,321

1865, when Edmund Kirby Smith surrenders in Texas. Some 1,556,000 soldiers fight for the Union, of whom 359,528 are killed in combat; of the approximately 850,000 Confederate troops, at least 225,000 are killed in combat.

1861

FEBRUARY 4 — In a convention at Montgomery, Alabama, the Confederate States of America is formed.

FEBRUARY 9 — Jefferson Davis, a hero of the Mexican War, congressman, senator, and former secretary of war, is elected provisional president of the Confederate States of America. He is inaugurated at Richmond, Virginia, on February 18.

APRIL 12, 4:30 A.M. — The first shots of the Civil War are fired when Confederate general Pierre Gustave Toutaint Beauregard begins an artillery bombardment of Fort Sumter, in Charleston Harbor. The fort falls to the Confederates the following day.

APRIL 19 — The Union commences its first major military operation against the Confederacy, a naval blockade of Southern ports. The army's aged and portly general-in-chief, Winfield Scott, claims the blockade will strangle the South as an anaconda strangles its prey. Criticized by many on both sides as impractical and even cowardly, the blockade is derided as "Scott's Anaconda." In fact, over time, it proves highly effective.

June 10 — Dorothea Dix, nationally renowned for her campaigns to reform the treatment of prisoners and asylum inmates, is appointed to oversee hospital nursing for the Union Army.

July 21 — The First Battle of Bull Run is fought near Manassas, Virginia. Confederate forces under P. G. T. Beauregard stun Northerners by defeating Union forces under Irvin McDowell. When one of the Confederate commanders, Thomas J. Jackson, holds the line against a critical Union assault, standing "like a stone wall," he earns the name by which he will be known throughout the rest of the war and to history: Stonewall Jackson.

1862

Congress creates the Department of Agriculture.

March 9 — Naval history is made during the Civil War when two ships of radical new design duel off the Virginia coast at Hampton Roads. The Union's all-iron *Monitor* fights the Confederacy's *Virginia,* an ironclad vessel created from the salvaged *Merrimack,* a Union ship of conventional design. These two vessels are the precursors of the modern battleship and herald the end of the era of wooden warships. Tactically, the battle is a draw, but because the *Virginia* is forced to withdraw, it ends in a strategic victory for the *Monitor.*

May 1 — Union naval captain David G. Farragut takes New Orleans in a spectacular run past the Confederate

Mississippi River forts. The loss of this vital port is crippling to the Confederacy.

MAY 20 — President Lincoln signs the Homestead Act, authorizing any citizen (or immigrant intending to become naturalized) to choose 160 acres of any surveyed but unclaimed parcel of public land, settle on it, improve it, and, by virtue of living on it for five years, take ownership of it. The Homestead Act opens up huge tracts of the West.

JULY — Maj. David Hunter organizes the Union's First Carolina Regiment, made up of the first African-American troops permitted to serve in the Union Army.

JULY 1 — Congress passes the Morrill Act "to punish and prevent the practice of polygamy in the territories." The law is directed against Mormon men, who at this time typically practice multiple-wife marriage.

JULY 1 — The Battle of Malvern Hill (Virginia) ends in a draw, bringing to a disappointing close the "Seven Days Campaign" of the Union's latest general-in-chief, George McClellan. The end of the Seven Days signals the failure of McClellan's larger Peninsula Campaign, designed to capture the Confederate capital of Richmond, Virginia. The Civil War will be longer and bloodier than anyone yet imagines.

AUGUST 18 — Little Crow, chief of the Minnesota Santee Sioux, begins a bloody uprising because promised federal subsidy payments and rations are withheld. For some five weeks, the Santee terrorize white Minnesota, killing perhaps 1,000 settlers before Col. Henry Sibley defeats Little Crow at the Battle of Wood Lake on September 23.

AUGUST 29–30 — The Second Battle of Bull Run is fought. The combination of generals Stonewall Jackson and Robert E. Lee defeats Union general John Pope, who retreats to nearby Washington, D.C.

SEPTEMBER 17 — The Battle of Antietam, near Sharpsburg, Maryland, is fought. This is the bloodiest single day of battle in the entire Civil War (each side suffers more than 2,000 killed and 9,000 wounded), ending in a very close Union victory.

SEPTEMBER 22 — Victory at Antietam, however narrow, emboldens Abraham Lincoln to issue a Preliminary Emancipation Proclamation. The document announces that, on January 1, 1863 (the date of the Final Emancipation Proclamation), all slaves within areas still in rebellion will be declared forever and irrevocably free. The Emancipation Proclamation frees no slaves in areas of the Confederacy occupied by Union forces as of January 1 nor slaves in the "border states" (Delaware, Maryland, Kentucky, and Missouri—slave states that did not secede) but it gives the Civil War greater moral urgency by defining it as a righteous war of liberation.

NOVEMBER 4 — Richard Jordan Gatling patents the Gatling gun. Precursor to the machine gun, it features six revolving barrels that provide very rapid fire. The Union Army does not adopt it until the Siege of Petersburg, late in the war (1864–1865).

DECEMBER 13 — Gen. Ambrose Burnside, chosen by Lincoln to replace McClellan as commander of the Army of the Potomac, leads his force to a terrible defeat at the Battle of Fredericksburg (Virginia). Burnside suffers 12,653 casualties, killed or wounded, compared to 5,300 for the Confederates.

1863

MARCH 3 — Congress passes the nation's first Conscription Act. Men between the ages of 20 and 45 are required to register for compulsory military service. The law favors the wealthy, since anyone capable of paying a $300 commutation fee (or hiring a substitute) can avoid conscription.

MAY 1–4 — Under "Fighting Joe" Hooker, who replaced Burnside after the Battle of Fredericksburg, the Union Army suffers another crushing defeat, this one at Chancellorsville, Virginia. It is Robert E. Lee's greatest victory, although the battle is very costly to both sides: More than 17,000 Union soldiers are killed or wounded, as are nearly 13,000 Confederates. The South also suffers the loss of Gen. Stonewall Jackson, killed when he becomes a victim of "friendly fire."

July 1–3 — The Union's Army of the Potomac, now under George G. Meade, intercepts Robert E. Lee's Army of Northern Virginia at the town of Gettysburg. Lee has invaded Pennsylvania, intending to break through Union forces so that he might advance against Washington. A three-day battle develops. The first day is one of Confederate advantage, but the Union forces hold out on July 2. On July 3, Lee orders a massive infantry charge ("Pickett's Charge") into the heart of the Union forces, suffers decisive defeat, and is forced to withdraw back into the Confederacy. Lee loses 30,000 killed or wounded, the North, 23,000. It is the turning point of the war, glorious and terrible.

July 4 — One day after Robert E. Lee is defeated at Gettysburg, the Mississippi River fortress city of Vicksburg, Mississippi, falls to Ulysses S. Grant. Deprived of the great river, the Confederacy is doomed to starve and strangle.

July 13–16 — Draft riots break out in New York City and in other cities of the North. The riots are, in large measure, racially motivated: poor laborers, most of them immigrants, do not want to fight to liberate slaves who (they believe) will take their jobs from them. In New York alone, about 1,000 persons are killed or wounded.

September 19–20 — William S. Rosecrans leads Union forces to defeat at the confusing wilderness battle of Chickamauga on the Georgia-Tennessee border. Both sides suffer about 25 percent casualties.

NOVEMBER 19 — Abraham Lincoln dedicates a military cemetery at the Gettysburg battlefield with the "Gettysburg Address." Just two minutes long, the speech eloquently defines the Union cause.

NOVEMBER 23–25 — Under a relentlessly systematic attack by Ulysses S. Grant, Confederate forces are defeated at the Battle of Chattanooga (Tennessee).

DECEMBER — Secretary of the Treasury Salmon P. Chase authorizes "In God We Trust" to be stamped on U.S. coins. The phrase becomes the official motto of the United States years later, in 1956.

DECEMBER 8 — President Lincoln issues an Amnesty Proclamation, offering a full pardon to all Southerners who take a "prescribed oath" of loyalty to the Union.

1864

CONGRESS AUTHORIZES the college division of the Columbia Institution for the Deaf, Dumb, and Blind in Washington, D.C., to grant degrees—the first higher educational opportunity given to the disabled. The school is renamed Gallaudet College in 1894 to honor Thomas Hopkins Gallaudet, a pioneer in the field of education for the deaf.

MARCH 10 — President Lincoln names Ulysses S. Grant general-in-chief of the Union Army. It is he, at long last, who will lead the Union forces to victory.

APRIL 12 — Confederate general Nathan Bedford Forrest captures Union-held Fort Pillow on the Mississippi River in Tennessee. The fort is garrisoned by 295 white troops of the 13th Tennessee Cavalry and 265 blacks of the 11th U.S. Colored Troops. Forrest leads or at least condones the deliberate killing of the African-American prisoners of war, only 62 of whom survive the "Fort Pillow Massacre."

MAY 5–6 — The armies of Ulysses S. Grant and Robert E. Lee duel in the Battle of the Wilderness outside of Chancellorsville, Virginia. Although no clear victor emerges, Grant continues his southward advance; whereas he is in a position to replace his losses, Lee cannot replenish his dwindling army.

MAY 12 — Union general Winfield Scott Hancock defeats Confederate forces at the Battle of Spotsylvania (Virginia), delivering another unrecoverable blow to the South.

JUNE 3 — Although vastly outnumbered 59,000 to 108,000, Robert E. Lee wins his last victory over Ulysses S. Grant at the Battle of Cold Harbor (Virginia). Between May 7 and June 3, the Union Army loses 50,000 men killed or wounded; the Confederacy suffers 32,000 losses. Despite the defeat, Grant continues his southerly advance.

JUNE 15–18 — General Grant begins the siege of Petersburg, Virginia. The siege, which will last nearly a year, marks the beginning of the final phase of the Civil War.

JUNE 30 — The Internal Revenue Act introduces an early form of federal income tax to help finance the war.

SEPTEMBER 1 — Grant's most important subordinate commander, William Tecumseh Sherman, captures Atlanta, the rail transportation nexus and industrial center of the Confederacy.

NOVEMBER 8 — The fall of Atlanta and other Civil War victories propel Abraham Lincoln to a second-term victory over Democrat (and former Union general) George B. McClellan in the presidential election.

NOVEMBER 16 — Having taken and then burned Atlanta, William Tecumseh Sherman begins his infamous "March to the Sea," intending to cause devastation sufficient to break the South's will to continue the war.

1864–1865

WITH THE army preoccupied in the East fighting the Civil War, the West is left highly vulnerable to Indian raids. During 1864–1865, the Cheyenne and Arapaho War rages fitfully.

1865

JOHN BATTERSON STETSON starts making hats in Philadelphia. His distinctive designs are based on styles he saw during travels in the American West, and they, in turn, come to define the iconic American "cowboy hat."

CLARA BARTON, who will found the American Red Cross in 1881, is hired by the U.S. government to direct efforts to locate missing soldiers. While performing this duty, she also distributes medical supplies to soldiers at the front and is widely looked upon as the "angel of the battlefield."

MARCH 3 — Congress creates the Freedman's Bureau to aid newly freed African Americans.

APRIL 9 — Gen. Robert E. Lee surrenders his Army of Northern Virginia to Ulysses S. Grant at Appomattox Court House, Virginia. This marks the effective (though unofficial) end of the Civil War.

APRIL 14 — In a conspiracy that includes a botched but bloody assassination attempt against Secretary of State William H. Seward and an aborted attempt against Vice President Andrew Johnson, John Wilkes Booth, a Maryland-born actor with Confederate sympathies, shoots Abraham Lincoln at Ford's Theatre in Washington, D.C. The president dies the next morning without regaining consciousness.

APRIL 15 — Following the assassination of Abraham Lincoln, Vice President Andrew Johnson—hard-drinking, uncouth, irascible, and highly unpopular—is sworn in as the nation's 17th president.

MAY 10 — Union troops capture Confederate president Jefferson Davis at Irwinville, Georgia. Imprisoned, he is indicted for treason, but is released on bail after serving two years. Charges are dropped in 1869, and Davis goes on to become president of the Carolina Life Insurance Company in Memphis, Tennessee.

MAY 29 — President Andrew Johnson issues an Amnesty Proclamation, which specifies classes of persons required to make special application for pardons.

OCTOBER — John Wesley Hyatt patents a celluloid billiard ball and lays claim to a $10,000 prize from a billiard ball manufacturer looking for a substitute for ivory. Hyatt's new substance lays the foundation of the plastics industry.

DECEMBER 18 — The 13th Amendment to the Constitution is ratified, prohibiting slavery in the United States.

DECEMBER 24 — The Ku Klux Klan is organized in the Pulaski, Tennessee, law office of Thomas M. Jones, a local judge. The name is derived from *kyklos,* the Greek word for circle, while the alliterative "klan" is almost certainly meant to appeal to the Scots-Irish descent of many Southerners. The organization does much to subvert Reconstruction efforts after the Civil War, eventually becoming a kind of shadow government throughout the South. In many places, its advocacy of white supremacy and the subjugation of former slaves results in acts of terrorism against African Americans, including murder.

1866

RECONSTRUCTION, THE process of reintegrating the former Confederate states into the Union, begins. It immediately threatens to divide the country anew. President Johnson favors lenient treatment for the South and proposes no special civil rights measures for the freed slaves. The radical wing of the Republican Party demands that the South be severely punished and calls for sweeping civil rights measures. The congressional election of 1866 brings in a radical Republican majority, which ensures a harsh, even punitive Reconstruction that creates much sectional and racial bitterness.

CHARLIE GOODNIGHT, a former Texas Ranger, teams up with cattleman Oliver Loving to blaze the Goodnight-Loving Trail from Texas to Colorado. Together, Goodnight and Loving invent the cattle drive and create the trail-drive industry, which in turn transforms the cowboy, a poorly paid agricultural worker, into an icon of American culture.

FEBRUARY 13 — Led by brothers Jesse and Frank James, both former Confederate guerrillas in Missouri, the James Gang robs its first bank, the Clay County Savings Association, netting a spectacular $60,000. At its peak, the James Gang consists of more than 40 outlaws; it commits violent robberies through 1881 and earns the Jameses an unmerited reputation as latter-day Robin Hoods. Many Americans mourn when Jesse James is shot and killed by a turncoat gang member, Robert Ford, on April 3, 1882.

APRIL 2 — President Johnson issues a proclamation declaring the "state of insurrection" to have ended. No other treaty or document certifies the end of the Civil War.

JULY 27 — A permanent trans-Atlantic cable is completed. The first cable, laid in 1858 but poorly insulated, had functioned for only three weeks before it failed.

1866–1868

RED CLOUD successfully leads the Oglala Sioux in resistance to white encroachment on Oglala lands in Montana and Wyoming along the Bozeman Trail. The 1867 Medicine Lodge Creek Treaty and 1868 Treaty of Fort Laramie end white use of the Bozeman Trail.

Seeking to end what they perceive as the invasion of their lands, the Snake (Northern Paiute) Indians attack settlers and miners in Oregon and Idaho. A combination of U.S. Army units and ad hoc militia forces defeat the Snake, who retreat to reservations.

1867

PURSUANT TO an order by Gen. William Tecumseh Sherman, Gen. Winfield Scott Hancock leads an expedition throughout Kansas and Nebraska to "punish" various Plains tribes for raids and other depredations. The result, called Hancock's War, is a military fiasco. The army pursues the Indians across the Great Plains; on the run, the Indians nevertheless continue to terrorize Kansas and Nebraska.

NEW YORK CITY enacts the Tenement House Law, which establishes minimum standards of space, light, ventilation, and construction for tenement housing. The law is important as the first housing law in America, but it is so poorly enforced that slum conditions in New York actually become worse.

HORATIO ALGER publishes the first of his "Ragged Dick" novels. Stories of poor boys who achieve great success through hard work, high ethics, and resistance to temptation, the novels are enormously popular versions of the boundlessly optimistic "American dream" and exert a profound influence on American popular culture during the 19th and early 20th centuries.

MARCH 2 — Congress passes the Tenure of Office Act, denying the president the unilateral authority to remove any official whose appointment was subject to the advice and consent of the Senate. Andrew Johnson's deliberate defiance of the act, which, he believes, is a threat to the constitutional system of checks and balances, precipitates his impeachment. The act eventually is declared unconstitutional in the 1926 case of *Myers* v. *United States.*

MARCH 30 — Secretary of State William Seward negotiates the purchase of Alaska from the czar of Russia for $7.2 million. Many mock the purchase as "Seward's Folly."

DECEMBER 4 — Oliver H. Kelley, a Minnesota farmer and member of the staff of the U.S. Department of Agriculture, founds the National Grange of the Patrons of Husbandry, headquartered in Washington, D.C. The Grange movement organizes the nation's farmers and gives them a political voice.

1868

GEORGE WESTINGHOUSE invents the air brake, which provides simultaneous and equal braking on all cars in a railroad train, thereby solving the most critical problem of rail safety and enabling explosive growth in the nation's rail network.

JANUARY 16 — Detroit fish dealer William Davis secures a patent for a refrigerated vehicle, an "icebox on wheels," to transport perishables. One year later, Davis patents the first refrigerated railroad car, an invention that transforms the commerce and business of agriculture.

MARCH 13 – MAY 26 — Congress conducts the impeachment trial of President Andrew Johnson for violating the Tenure of Office Act (passed March 2, 1867). The true motive for the impeachment is Johnson's opposition to the radical Republican program of punitive Reconstruction. The trial begins on March 13. On May 26, 35 senators vote to convict, 19 to acquit, coming up one vote short of the two-thirds majority required to remove Johnson from office.

JULY 9 — The 14th Amendment is ratified, explicitly and irrevocably granting citizenship to all those born or naturalized in the United States, including the slaves freed by the Civil War and the 13th Amendment. The amendment also denies state and federal responsibility for debts incurred in aid of the rebellion against the United States.

NOVEMBER 3 — Republican Ulysses S. Grant, hero of the Union in the Civil War, is elected president. His popular majority over Democrat Horatio Seymour is a slim 306,000 votes, and it is clear that the new African-American vote, some 700,000 ballots in this election, is responsible for his victory.

1868–1869

WILLIAM TECUMSEH SHERMAN, now in command of all western U.S. Army forces, dispatches Philip H. Sheridan to wage total war against the Cheyenne and allied tribes in western Kansas and eastern Colorado. "Sheridan's Campaign" destroys shelter and sustenance, forcing the Indians to retreat to Indian Territory and other reservations. In January 1869, Sheridan holds a conference with 50 Indian chiefs at Fort Cobb, Indian Territory. When the Comanche chief Toch-a-way is introduced to Sheridan, he says, "Me Toch-a-way, me good Indian." The general replies, "The only good Indians I ever saw were dead"— a remark that makes its way into American popular culture as "The only good Indian is a dead Indian."

1869

FEBRUARY 6 — *Harper's Weekly* publishes Thomas Nast's first caricature of Uncle Sam to personify the U.S. government.

The Uncle Sam figure may have appeared as early as the War of 1812, but Nast's version becomes a universal American symbol.

MAY 10 — In a ceremony at Promontory Summit (not Promontory Point, as many histories erroneously record), 56 miles west of Ogden, Utah, Leland Stanford, chief executive of the Central Pacific Railroad, drives a golden spike into the track, joining the eastbound rails of the Central Pacific to the westbound rails of the Union Pacific and completing the first American transcontinental railroad.

MAY 15 — Elizabeth Cady Stanton and Susan B. Anthony found the National Woman Suffrage Association, the most prominent of several organizations campaigning to obtain voting rights for women.

SEPTEMBER 24 — Wall Street's "Black Friday" triggers a national financial panic, the result of failed attempts by financiers Jay Gould and James Fisk to corner the gold market. The episode demonstrates the volatility of America's entirely unregulated boom-or-bust economy in the so-called Gilded Age following the Civil War.

DECEMBER 10 — Wyoming Territory grants women the right to vote, becoming the first American jurisdiction to permit woman suffrage. The 19th Amendment, ensuring the right constitutionally, won't be ratified for 51 more years.

1870

JOHN D. ROCKEFELLER forms the Standard Oil Company. Under his direction, the company grows into a powerful vertical monopoly, controlling not only the extraction of oil but also industries involved in the refinement of crude oil, the transportation of petroleum products, and the sale and distribution of those products. Standard Oil becomes American big business at its biggest and is the predecessor company of today's ExxonMobil Corporation.

FEBRUARY 25 — Hiram R. Revels, a Republican from Mississippi, becomes the first African American in Congress when he takes his Senate seat.

MARCH 30 — Congress adopts the 15th Amendment, barring states from depriving citizens of the right to vote because of race, color, or "previous condition of servitude." Conspicuously absent from this list is "gender."

JUNE 22 — Congress creates the U.S. Department of Justice, headed by the U.S. attorney-general. The department is the first central law enforcement administrative agency in the federal government.

1871

MARCH 3 — Congress passes the Indian Appropriation Act, by which all treaties made between the United States and Indian tribes are summarily nullified and Native Americans become wards of the federal government.

MARCH 4 — President Grant creates the Civil Service Commission. Its purpose is to transform the basis of government appointments from political patronage and cronyism to the merit of the appointee, fairly and objectively determined. Congress, whose members relish patronage as a means of acquiring and consolidating their power, denies the commission adequate funding, so that it proves mostly ineffectual.

SEPTEMBER 4 — An investigation by a New York City citizens commission begins into the massive corruption of "Tammany Hall," the executive committee of the Democratic Party in New York City, led by William Marcy "Boss" Tweed. Tweed, the most flamboyant and daring of the nation's many corrupt "Gilded Age" city "bosses," is arrested at the end of 1871 and convicted on November 19, 1873. An era of political reform is gradually introduced throughout urban America.

OCTOBER 8 — The Great Chicago Fire begins when a cow kicks over a lantern in Patrick O'Leary's (*not* Mrs. O'Leary's) DeKoven Street barn on the city's shabby working-class West Side. The fire quickly spreads, engulfing 2,124 acres, destroying 17,500 buildings, killing 250 persons, and rendering 98,500 homeless before it burns itself out on October 11. Among the treasures lost in the blaze is Abraham Lincoln's original draft of the Emancipation Proclamation. The nation's most promising new generation of architects, including Daniel Burnham and Louis Sullivan, immediately begins designing magnificent buildings that will not only resurrect Chicago but transform it into a center of modern American urban architecture.

1872

A. MONTGOMERY WARD, a prominent Chicago merchant, begins distributing a 280-page catalog throughout the rural Midwest, thereby giving farmers an opportunity to purchase, by mail order, merchandise from his dry goods emporium. In 1889, noting the success of Ward's mail-order operation, Richard W. Sears and A. C. Roebuck begin their own catalog-based mail-order business, which grows into the giant of the industry. The exponential growth of Internet retailing at the end of the 20th century will take the catalog mail-order model to yet another transformative level.

MASSIVE CORRUPTION and fraud are exposed in Crédit Moblier, the company formed by the directors of the Union Pacific Railroad to finance construction of the transcontinental rail line. The scandal comes to a head with the public exposure of businessmen and politicians, including highly placed officials of President Grant's administration. Crédit Moblier is revealed as a company run by the directors of the Union Pacific and paid by the Union Pacific to build the Union Pacific. Because the directors (principal investors) profit from the railroad as well as from the cost of building it, they

U.S. POPULATION: 39,818,449

routinely inflate the costs Crédit Moblier charges to the railroad, masking everything with an elaborate shell game the likes of which will not be seen in America until the Enron corporate debacle at the start of the 21st century.

MARCH 1 — President Grant signs legislation creating the Yellowstone National Park Reserve, the first federally owned land to be set aside specifically for the enjoyment of the public.

NOVEMBER 5 — Despite widespread corruption, President Grant wins reelection, soundly defeating Democrat Horace Greeley.

1873

MARCH 3 — Anthony Comstock, secretary of the Society for the Suppression of Vice, successfully agitates for passage of an act prohibiting obscene materials from being sent through the U.S. mails. The "Comstock Act" becomes the basis for a wide range of attempts at censorship and the imposition of straitlaced conservative morality throughout the nation.

OCTOBER 27 — Joseph Glidden of Illinois patents the first commercially successful barbed wire, providing the practical means by which the open spaces of the western prairies and plains can be divided and subdivided. As many see it, the new invention, for better or worse, "tames" the vast and wild Plains country.

NOVEMBER — The Woman's Christian Temperance Union (WCTU) is founded in Cleveland, Ohio, and becomes the organizing force behind a rapidly growing nationwide alcohol prohibition movement.

1874–1875

KIOWA AND COMANCHE raids against white settlers in Texas and Kansas, on the border of Indian Territory (principally modern Oklahoma), prompt Gen. William T. Sherman to authorize a major campaign dubbed the "Red River War." After bitter fighting, the militant Kwahadi Comanche agree, for the first time in their history, to retire to a reservation.

1875

MAY 17 — The first Kentucky Derby is run at Churchill Downs, Louisville, Kentucky. Oliver Lewis rides Aristides to victory with a time of 2:37:25. The Derby becomes one of the most famous annual sporting events in the nation.

1876

MARCH 7 — Alexander Graham Bell receives patent no. 174,465, for what is modestly captioned an "improvement in telegraphy." It is, in fact, the first practical telephone, an epoch-making means of transmitting the human voice over distance by wire.

NOVEMBER 7 — The presidential election gives Democrat Samuel J. Tilden a plurality victory over Republican Rutherford B. Hayes, but Republicans dispute returns in

Florida, Louisiana, South Carolina, and Oregon; manipulating the Reconstruction governments they control, they steal the election by reversing the electoral tallies in the three Southern states. This throws the presidential contest into the House of Representatives, which appoints a 15-member electoral commission to determine the winner. In secret negotiations, the Democrats agree to allow a Republican majority on the commission (thereby ensuring Hayes's election) in return for a Republican pledge that Hayes will immediately end Reconstruction, removing the military-controlled state governments that have ruled the South since the end of the Civil War and allowing the predominantly Democratic Southern states to form their own popularly elected governments. Hayes accordingly assumes office and Reconstruction abruptly ends, but the president is universally mocked with the title "Your Fraudulency" and wisely chooses not to run for a second term.

JUNE 25 — George Armstrong Custer, the colorful "boy general" of the Civil War and now the flamboyant commander of the U.S. Seventh Cavalry, leads part of his 600-man force against a Sioux camp on the Little Bighorn River in eastern Montana Territory and is overwhelmed by a massive counterattack led by Crazy Horse and others. Custer is killed with all 262 troopers engaged in the battle. Custer, a reckless and brutal commander, becomes for many Americans a hero and martyr in what is called the struggle of civilization against savagery. For Native Americans, he is a symbol of genocidal ruthlessness.

1876–1877

THE GREAT SIOUX WAR is fought over possession of the Black Hills in the Dakota Territory. The hills are sacred to the Sioux and Cheyenne, but are also coveted by white prospectors after gold is discovered in them. Following bitter resistance led by such legendary figures as the Oglala chief Crazy Horse and Sitting Bull, a Hunkpapa Sioux, the Indians either withdraw to reservations or flee to Canada.

1876–1886

THE APACHE, whose heritage is one of raiding and warfare, violently resist confinement to reservations. For a decade, the U.S. Army fights to round up the Apache, whose most determined and skilled war leader is Geronimo. Long after other Indians give up, Geronimo does not surrender until September 4, 1886, having led large numbers of U.S. troops in a pursuit throughout the American Southwest and deep into Mexico. His surrender marks the end of the great Apache War.

1877

MARCH 5 — Within a month after the inauguration of Rutherford B. Hayes, Reconstruction ends throughout the South. Freed of federal supervision and military control, the Southern states enact legislation that relegates African Americans to a permanent underclass status.

JUNE–OCTOBER 5 — When Chief Joseph the Younger of the Nez Perce refuses to relinquish lands coveted by white settlers, the U.S. Army, beginning in June, pursues his tribe over 1,500 miles through portions of Idaho, Washington, Oregon, and Montana, seeking to prevent their escape to Canada, where they could unite with exiled Sioux under Sitting Bull and return in force to the United States. The pursuit ends at the Battle of Bear Paw Mountain on October 5. Forced to surrender most of his tribe, Joseph declares "I am tired; my heart is sick and sad. From where the sun now stands I will fight no more forever." Joseph's eloquence is an elegy on the fate of the Native American after 400 years of contact with Europeans, Euro-Americans, and the forces of the United States.

NOVEMBER 29 — Thomas Alva Edison demonstrates the phonograph, a remarkably simple device for recording sound. He files for a patent on December 15. Many of the inventor's contemporaries regard it as his most miraculous invention, a machine that seems to preserve passing time itself.

1878

AMERICAN PHYSICIST Albert A. Michelson publishes a paper, "On a Method of Measuring the Velocity of Light," which leads to further work that forms the background against which Albert Einstein creates the Theory of Special Relativity in 1905. Although the United States is noted for its inventors and technologists, Michelson is the nation's first internationally recognized advanced theoretician.

JANUARY 1 — The Knights of Labor are formed as the first national union to attempt to unite all labor in a single great organization.

FEBRUARY — Born Henry McCarty (not, as many believe, William Bonney) in 1859, "Billy the Kid" receives his baptism of fire during the Lincoln County War, a range war—a violent dispute between rival cattle interests— that begins in February and ends in a four-day gun battle in July. He emerges from the struggle a confirmed outlaw at age 19, making his living through armed robbery. Billy is solely responsible for killing four men and takes part in the killing of five more during a brief career of crime cut short by Sheriff Pat Garrett, who guns him down on July 14, 1881. Active only three years, Billy is widely remembered not as a young thug, thief, and murderer but as a gallant lost soul, living by his outlaw wits and defying the forces of a corrupt and repressive society.

1879

MARY BAKER EDDY organizes the Church of Christ, Scientist in Lynn, Massachusetts. Eddy regards Christian Science as a universal, practical system of spiritual, prayer-based healing.

JANUARY 27 — Thomas Alva Edison patents the first practical incandescent electric lamp. More than any other single invention of the 19th century, the electric light transforms modern civilization.

OCTOBER 6 — The Carlisle Indian School, founded by Richard Henry Pratt, opens in Carlisle, Pennsylvania, to provide Native Americans with a basic education. Founded as an elementary school, the institution develops into an industrial high school and teacher's college before it is abandoned in 1918.

1880

MARCH 1 — In *Struader* v. *West Virginia*, the Supreme Court holds that the exclusion of African Americans from juries is unconstitutional.

NOVEMBER 2 — James A. Garfield is elected president, defeating Democrat Winfield Scott Hancock.

NOVEMBER 17 — The United States concludes with China the so-called Chinese Exclusion Treaty. The treaty gives the United States the right to "regulate, limit, or suspend" Chinese immigration into the country, provided that Chinese nationals are not completely or permanently barred.

1881

MAY 21 — Inspired by the example of the International Committee of the Red Cross in Europe, Clara Barton, the Civil War's "angel of the battlefield," founds the American Red Cross to provide large-scale aid in times of war and major natural disasters.

JULY 2 — President Garfield is shot in Washington, D.C., by Charles J. Guiteau, a disappointed and deranged office seeker. The wounded Garfield lingers for months, finally succumbing to infection on September 19, without ever having left his bed. Vice President Chester A. Arthur is inaugurated.

JULY 4 — Founded in February by African-American educator Booker T. Washington, the Tuskegee Institute opens in Tuskegee, Alabama. Created mainly as a modest vocational school—Washington believed that blacks would achieve social equality only if they first became economically self-supporting and successful—Tuskegee gradually evolves into a major African-American university.

SEPTEMBER 4 — Thomas Alva Edison builds and opens the world's first electric generating plant in Lower Manhattan on Pearl Street. As Edison had planned, his electric light creates a demand for electricity, and he quite accurately envisions the day when electric power will be universally supplied throughout the world.

1882

FEBRUARY 7 — John L. Sullivan defeats Paddy Ryan at Mississippi City, Mississippi, to win the world heavyweight boxing championship. Sullivan is on his way to becoming a national sports hero—and to elevating prize fighting to the level of a respectable and profitable professional sport.

1883

MAY 24 — The Brooklyn Bridge opens, construction having begun in 1869. Designed by John Roebling and completed after his death (due to a construction accident) by his son Washington Roebling, the bridge combines cutting-edge suspension engineering with an architectural style that recalls a Gothic cathedral. It is, in fact, a cathedral for the modern age, a monument to 19th-century American technology, ingenuity, courage, and will.

NOVEMBER 18 — The expansion of the railway network across the North American continent prompts railroads to adopt a system of Standard Time in the United States and Canada, creating and standardizing time zones. In 1884, the system is expanded at an international conference and applied on a worldwide basis.

NOVEMBER 29 — The first national college football championship game is played. Yale wins over Harvard, 23–2.

1884

SAMUEL LANGHORNE CLEMENS, a Missouri-born humorist, novelist, and former riverboat pilot—whose pen name, Mark Twain, is derived from the call of the riverboat leadsman signaling a safe navigational depth of two fathoms—publishes his masterpiece, *Adventures of Huckleberry Finn*. The story of a boy's coming of age in pre–Civil War America, the novel vividly depicts both the nobility and depravity of humanity in the microcosm of life along the great Mississippi River. Many literary historians regard it as the very greatest of American novels.

U.S. POPULATION: 50,156,000

AUGUST 26 — German-born American inventor Ottmar Mergenthaler patents the Linotype, a machine capable of forming an entire line of printing type as a single piece of metal. The Linotype greatly speeds and economizes the process of producing books and newspapers and revolutionizes not only printing but the entire information industry.

NOVEMBER 4 — Democrat Grover Cleveland is elected president, defeating Republican James G. Blaine.

1885

FEBRUARY 25 — Congress upholds the principle that public lands are to be reserved for public use by passing legislation to prohibit the fencing of public lands in the West.

1886

MAY 4 — A bomb explodes at a labor rally held in Chicago's Haymarket Square, killing eight police officers and four civilians and wounding others. Anarchists are blamed, and the event is condemned as the "Haymarket Riot." Eight men, self-confessed anarchists, are brought to trial, and, in a rush to judgment among a population terrified by anarchy, Judge Joseph E. Gary imposes death sentence on seven of them (the eighth is given 15 years in prison), even though none of the accused is directly linked to the bombing. Four are hanged, one commits suicide, and the sentences of two are commuted to imprisonment for life. On June 26, 1893, Illinois governor John Peter Altgeld pardons the three who are still in the penitentiary; his action, courageous and unpopular, destroys his political career.

MAY 10 — In *Yick Wo* v. *Hopkins,* the Supreme Court declares municipal ordinances discriminating against Chinese laundries unconstitutional and, most importantly, declares that aliens are persons under the law, entitled to all the legal rights of persons.

OCTOBER 28 — Grover Cleveland presides at the dedication of the Statue of Liberty. Created by French sculptor Frédéric-Auguste Bartholdi—who reportedly modeled the 151-foot copper statue on his mother—the monument is a gift of the French people and commemorates the two nations' common struggle on behalf of democracy, liberty, and justice over the previous century. For generations of immigrants, the statue comes to symbolize the ideal of freedom and the promise of a better life in America.

DECEMBER 8 — The American Federation of Labor is founded, with Samuel Gompers as its first president. The organization brings together a range of skilled-labor unions into a politically powerful force.

1887

DURING THIS YEAR — the apex of an era of monopolistic "trusts" that characterize what many call America's greed-driven "Gilded Age"—86 new monopolistic business enterprises are created.

THE FOXBURG GOLF CLUB, Foxburg, Pennsylvania, is opened by John Mickle Fox. It is generally considered the first golf club in the United States.

FEBRUARY 8 — Congress passes the Dawes Severalty Act. The legislation dismantles the Indian reservation system by allotment of tribal lands to individual Indian ownership. Ostensibly, the act is motivated by the belief that individual ownership will stimulate the Indians' will to succeed in American capitalistic society; however, by removing the protection afforded by collective reservation status, the act makes Indian lands available for purchase and thereby continues the process by which Native Americans have been progressively divested of their holdings. By the time the law is overturned in 1934, Indian-held land consists of just 48,000,000 acres, down from the 138,000,000 in 1887.

1888

GEORGE EASTMAN introduces the "Kodak No. 1," a simple and inexpensive box camera that brings photography to the masses who document their everyday lives in a multitude of "snapshots."

JUNE 13 — Congress creates the U.S. Department of Labor, reflecting the growing influence of the national labor movement. The new department does not attain cabinet-level status until March 4, 1913.

NOVEMBER 6 — Louisville, Kentucky, becomes the first municipality to adopt the "Australian ballot": voting by secret ballot. In 1950, South Carolina becomes the last state to adopt the system, making it national in scope.

NOVEMBER 6 — Benjamin Harrison is elected president, defeating Grover Cleveland's bid for a second term.

1889

SOCIAL ACTIVIST Jane Addams founds Hull House in a Chicago slum. This "settlement house," modeled after London's Toynbee Hall, in turn becomes the model for similar establishments in other American cities. Here poor immigrants are helped to "fit into" American society, and slum dwellers are given opportunities to learn English, acquire trade skills, and generally improve their education and, thereby, their lot in life.

J. WALKER FEWKES makes sound recordings of Indian speech and music, first in Maine and, later, throughout the Southwest.

JONES & LAUGHLIN, a Pittsburgh steel manufacturer, begins turning out I beams, the basic structural elements of the new mode of steel-skeleton construction. The I beam makes skyscrapers possible.

APRIL 22 — At noon, a pistol shot signals the beginning of the great Oklahoma Land Rush, as the federal government opens 1.9 million acres of formerly Indian land to settlement. Would-be homesteaders race one another to stake their claims.

MAY 31 — When the dam above Johnstown, Pennsylvania, fails, 2,209 or more die in the great Johnstown Flood.

JULY 8 — The firm of Dow Jones & Company commences publication of the four-page daily *Wall Street Journal.* Specializing in news immediately relevant to investors and other members of the financial community, the newspaper rapidly grows into a publication of great influence and authority.

1890

THE LEGENDARY NEW ORLEANS cornetist and bandleader Buddy Bolden is credited by many with inventing jazz or, at least, laying its foundation. Virtually all of the first generation of New Orleans jazz musicians play with Bolden's band early in their careers.

NEW YORK journalist Jacob Riis publishes *How the Other Half Lives,* a combination of text and stark photographs documenting life in the city's teeming Lower East Side slums. The book spurs legislation aimed at slum clearance and general urban social reform.

INNOVATIVE CHICAGO-BASED architect Louis Sullivan pioneers the development of the "skyscraper" with the Wainwright Building in St. Louis. Thanks to Sullivan and architects inspired by his example, the skyscraper becomes the dominant commercial building type of the modern American urban scene. Sullivan's buildings are not only innovative but also beautiful, replacing fussy and merely decorative styles with an exciting "form follows function" aesthetic.

MISSISSIPPI BECOMES the first state to incorporate into its constitution restrictions on black suffrage by requiring a literacy test as a qualification for voting. A "grandfather clause" exempts from the test those who had the right to vote prior to 1866 and the lineal descendants of such persons. Although most Southern African Americans as well as many Southern whites are illiterate during this period, the grandfather clause exemption applies exclusively to whites because no black man in the South had the right to vote before 1866.

APRIL 14 — The United States and the other nations of the hemisphere form the Pan-American Union, an affirmation of the political solidarity of the Americas. Created to advance international cooperation, the Union offers technical and informational services to all the American republics, serves as a repository for international documents, and generally promotes economic, social, juridical, and cultural relations.

JULY 2 — Congress passes the Sherman Antitrust Act. The law declares illegal "every...trust...or conspiracy...in restraint of trade or commerce among the several States, or with foreign nations" and is aimed at ending the economic tyranny of monopolistic giants.

JULY 14 — Congress passes the Sherman Silver Act, which seeks to stabilize currency by requiring the government to purchase 4.5 million ounces of silver each month and to issue currency in the form of silver certificates against it. The act is repealed in 1893.

OCTOBER 1 — The McKinley Tariff is passed by Congress, bringing protectionism to the highest levels yet by charging formidable duties on most imported manufactured goods.

DECEMBER 15 — Sitting Bull, the most important leader of the Sioux and a chief of great political and spiritual authority, is killed in a scuffle with Native American reservation police who, acting on the orders of white authorities, attempt to arrest him.

DECEMBER 29 — Soldiers of the Seventh Cavalry surround the camp of the Miniconjou Sioux chief Big Foot at Wounded Knee Creek on the Pine Ridge Reservation in South Dakota. While in the process of confiscating the Indians' weapons, a fight breaks out, and cavalry troopers open up on the Indians with rapid-fire Hotchkiss guns. After the Wounded Knee Massacre, the bodies of Big Foot and 153 other Miniconjou are found, but it is likely that a total of 300 lost their lives. Two weeks after Wounded Knee, on January 15, 1891, the Sioux nation formally surrenders to U.S. Army officials, marking the end of 400 years of warfare between whites and Indians in the Americas.

1891

LOOKING FOR a means of improving attendance at YMCAs during the winter, Dr. James Naismith, an instructor at the YMCA International Training School in Springfield, Massachusetts, invents an entirely new indoor game. "Basketball" uses a ball and two peach baskets as goals. To suit it to indoor play, players are not allowed to tackle or otherwise make contact with one another, and they are not allowed to run with the ball. The game develops into one of the most popular in the United States—for children, amateurs, and high school and college players, as well as for highly paid professionals.

MARCH 4 — Congress passes the first International Copyright Act. Initially, the act protects the work of British, French, Belgian, and Swiss authors, preventing their books from being pirated by U.S. publishers. The act becomes the basis for a series of worldwide copyright acts and international conventions and is a major step in the recognition of the value of intellectual property.

MAY 5 — Carnegie Hall, destined to become the nation's most exalted performance space for classical music, opens at 57th Street and Seventh Avenue in New York City. Construction has been funded by steel magnate Andrew Carnegie, America's leading philanthropist.

SEPTEMBER — The Duryea brothers, Charles and Frank— bicycle mechanics and toolmakers from Chicopee,

U.S. POPULATION: 62,948,000

Massachusetts—successfully test the first gasoline-powered automobile built in the United States.

1892

THE BOLL WEEVIL, a beetle from Mexico and Central America, arrives in the United States and infests cotton country from Texas eastward. It causes great devastation to the South's staple cash crop and cripples the region's economy, but it also forces Southern farmers to begin to diversify their crops, ultimately contributing to the improved development of Southern agriculture in the long term.

FRANK LLOYD WRIGHT, destined to become America's most famous modern architect, designs his first building, the Charnley House in Chicago. Wright goes on to develop the "Prairie style," exemplified in Chicago's magnificent Robey House (1907), which features a broad, low roof, strong horizontal lines, and harmonious integration of design elements inside and out.

JANUARY 1 — Ellis Island opens in upper New York Bay as the principal receiving and processing station for immigrants arriving via the Atlantic. Before it closes on November 12, 1954, Ellis Island processes more than 20 million immigrants.

MAY 5 — Congress renews the Chinese Exclusion Act with the Geary Act, which mandates strict registration of all Chinese workers and the deportation of workers not authorized to remain.

MAY 28 — California naturalist John Muir merges a group of citizens organized to protect the Sierra Nevada against rampant commercial exploitation with the Alpine Club, a University of California mountaineering group, to form the Sierra Club, the nation's first (and now oldest) environmental advocacy organization.

JUNE 26 — Workers strike the Homestead Steel Plant in Pittsburgh to protest wage cuts by Carnegie Steel and the company's refusal to recognize the workers' union. Company officials bring in Pinkerton agents—private police thugs—to break up the strike, and the strike explodes into violence. The Pinkerton men retreat after three of their number are killed and more wounded. Ten strikers die. At the company's request, the state of Pennsylvania supplies militia forces to protect strike-breakers who keep the plant running. On November 20, the strikers surrender, the union is destroyed, and many of the strikers lose their jobs. It is a dark day for organized labor and is symptomatic of the labor unrest that is widespread throughout the nation during this period.

AUGUST 4 — Andrew J. Borden and his second wife, Abby, are murdered in their Fall River, Massachusetts, home. The weapon is an axe. The prime suspect is their spinster daughter, Lisbeth "Lizzie" Borden. Her trial rivets the nation, and although she is acquitted for lack of compelling evidence, many consider her guilty, as conveyed in a popular children's song of the day: "Lizzie Borden took an axe, / Gave her mother 40 whacks. / When she saw what she had done, / She gave her father 41."

OCTOBER 20–23 — The World's Columbian Exposition is dedicated in Chicago to showcase American technology and business. Its official opening day is May 1, 1893, just four days before the devastating financial Panic of 1893 begins to sweep the nation.

NOVEMBER 8 — Grover Cleveland is elected president, the first (and so far only) U.S. president elected to a second nonconsecutive term. He defeats incumbent Benjamin Harrison by a wide margin.

1893

JANUARY 17 — The United States supports a revolution in Hawaii that deposes Queen Liliuokalani. This is followed by a hastily negotiated Hawaiian Annexation Treaty, which is submitted to the Senate on February 15, only to be withdrawn over questions about the propriety of U.S. actions.

MAY 5 — Stocks plummet on the New York Stock Exchange, signaling the start of a nationwide financial panic as foreign investors withdraw U.S. investments, railroads go bankrupt, the steel industry retreats sharply, and banks begin to fail in alarming numbers. Fifteen thousand firms collapse, 500 banks go into receivership, one-third of the nation's railroads become insolvent, and about 20 percent of the workforce is suddenly unemployed. Riots and fears of revolution sweep the country, which sinks into a financial depression that does not end until 1897.

JULY 12 — History professor Frederick Jackson Turner of the University of Wisconsin delivers a speech as part of the World's Columbian Exposition in Chicago in which he presents census statistics that reveal the "closing" of the American frontier—that is, the population figures no longer demarcate a distinct western limit of settlement. Turner declares that the "restless, nervous energy...dominant individualism...buoyancy and exuberance" traditionally engendered in the American character by the presence of the frontier will now be channeled into ventures abroad and the United States will enter an age of imperialism.

1894

MARCH 17 — A new Chinese Exclusion Treaty is signed, by which China agrees to the exclusion of most Chinese laborers from the United States in exchange for guarantees that Chinese persons currently living in the country will enjoy "the same rights, privileges, immunities and exemptions as may be enjoyed by the citizens or subjects of the most favored nation" and that the exclusion will be applied only to laborers and not to Chinese "of other classes," such as professionals and businessmen.

MARCH 25 — Businessman Jacob S. Coxey leads a march of 100 unemployed men from Massillon, Ohio, bound for Washington, D.C. His plan is to gather more marchers en route and appeal to Congress to authorize an ambitious program of public works—financed by an increase of the money in circulation—to provide jobs for the unemployed. "Coxey's Army" arrives in Washington on April 30, having grown to 500 men—but far short of the thousands Coxey had envisioned. Coxey and his men are arrested on May 1 for trespassing on the Capitol lawn, and the protest disintegrates. Coxey later leads a second "army" in 1914, with similarly disappointing results.

MAY 11 — Workers strike against the Pullman railroad car plant south of Chicago. George M. Pullman owns the company for which his workers labor; he owns the town—Pullman, Illinois—in which they are required to live; he owns the houses and tenements they rent; and, he owns the stores from which they buy their food, clothing, and other necessities. The strike is triggered by sharp wage reductions imposed by Pullman without concomitant reductions in rents and company store prices. Violence erupts and triggers a nationwide railroad strike in sympathy with the plight of the Pullman workers.

JUNE 28 — Congress passes a resolution creating Labor Day to recognize and honor the working man.

JULY 2 — National labor leader Eugene V. Debs is convicted of criminal contempt for his role in the Pullman strike. Clarence Darrow, the nation's most celebrated defense attorney, represents Debs at the trial, beginning on

December 14, 1893, and leads the charge against the use of blanket injunctions intended to suppress labor protests.

AUGUST 8 — Retreating from its earlier move to annex Hawaii, the United States officially recognizes the new Hawaiian Republic, but extends the Monroe Doctrine to cover it, warning foreign powers that any interference in Hawaiian affairs will be regarded as an assault on U.S. sovereignty.

AUGUST 27 — Congress enacts the first graduated income tax, a controversial measure that is declared unconstitutional the following year.

SEPTEMBER 4 — Twelve thousand New York City garment workers strike to protest sweatshop work conditions and the ruinous piecework system of payment, by which workers are paid not for their time but for each piece of work they turn out.

1895

NEW YORK journalist, short-story writer, and novelist Stephen Crane publishes *The Red Badge of Courage,* a novel of the Civil War so realistic that many mistake it for a nonfiction documentary memoir. Crane's work represents the apex of American literary realism in fiction.

AUGUST 31 — The first professional football game is played in Latrobe, Pennsylvania, with the local team pitted against a team from Jeannette, Pennsylvania. Players share the profits; however, Latrobe pays substitute quarterback John Brailler $10 to cover his expenses, making him, according to historians of the sport, football's first true professional player because he is paid directly and separately.

NOVEMBER 28 — The nation's first race of gasoline-powered automobiles is run between Chicago and Evanston, Illinois, on Thanksgiving Day.

1896

CHICAGO NEWSPAPERMAN Finley Peter Dunne creates "Mr. Dooley," a fictional Irish saloonkeeper who becomes a phenomenally successful vehicle for wry observations about the political and social scene and sets the standard for humorous political commentary in the United States.

MAY 18 — In *Plessy* v. *Ferguson,* the Supreme Court upholds as constitutional segregationist laws that mandate "separate but equal" public accommodations for whites and blacks. The decision becomes the legal basis for the segregation of public facilities and schools in the South.

JULY 11 — Presidential nominee William Jennings Bryan of Nebraska delivers his famous "Cross of Gold" speech to the Democratic National Convention. Vowing not to "crucify" the American people on a "cross of gold," Bryan espouses the party platform of free and unlimited coinage of both silver and gold at the rate of 16 silver coins to each gold coin. The Republican Party, in contrast, advocates a strict gold standard for the United States.

AUGUST 12 — Gold is discovered on the Klondike River in the Canadian Yukon, sparking the second great American gold rush as thousands make the arduous journey to the Canadian Northwest.

OCTOBER 1 — The U.S. Postal Service inaugurates Rural Free Delivery (RFD) service—free postal delivery service for rural customers—which does much to end the physical, cultural, economic, and intellectual isolation of American farming communities, as well as promoting the building of new roads and to spurring the development of the mail-order retail industry.

NOVEMBER 3 — William McKinley is elected president, defeating Democrat William Jennings Bryan.

1898

DR. CARL A. SCHENK establishes the Biltmore Forest School in Biltmore, North Carolina, bringing European forest-husbandry techniques to the United States. Although the school closes in 1913, it is a major step in the U.S. conservation movement.

FEBRUARY 15 — The battleship USS *Maine* explodes in the harbor of Havana, Cuba, with the loss of 260 sailors. A naval board of inquiry attributes the loss to a Spanish mine, and war fever rapidly rises in the United States.

(Subsequent investigation long after the Spanish-American War traces the actual cause of the explosion to the accidental detonation of the *Maine's* powder magazine and not to any Spanish action.)

APRIL 24–AUGUST 12 — The Spanish-American War is fought. Ostensibly, the cause of war is Spain's oppression of its colony Cuba and a putative Spanish military threat to the United States. The more compelling cause is the desire of the United States to acquire territory at the expense of Spain and to ensure the profitable security of extensive American business interests in the Caribbean.

MAY 1 — In the naval Battle of Manila Bay, U.S. commodore George Dewey scores a one-sided victory against the larger but less modern Spanish fleet anchored in Manila Bay, Philippines. Eight U.S. sailors are wounded, whereas the Spanish fleet is utterly destroyed. The action clears the way for U.S. occupation of Manila and, ultimately, annexation of the Spanish-held Philippines.

MAY 7 — While the United States exercises its imperial ambitions in Cuba and the Philippines, Congress jointly resolves to annex Hawaii. President McKinley signs the congressional resolution on July 7.

JUNE 21 — Spanish-held Guam surrenders to the United States, and this island in the Pacific Marianas group becomes a U.S. possession.

JULY 1–2 — U.S. troops, including the all-volunteer Rough Riders regiment led by Theodore Roosevelt, storm Spanish strong points in Cuba at El Caney and San Juan Heights. The American victory ensures the defeat of the Spanish on Cuba, and Roosevelt emerges from the battle a popular American hero in the mold of Andrew Jackson.

JULY 3 — The U.S. Navy engages the Spanish fleet at Santiago, Cuba. As at Manila Bay, the Cuban-based fleet is almost entirely destroyed.

JULY 25 — Maj. Gen. Nelson Appleton Miles leads a U.S. invasion of Spanish-held Puerto Rico and, meeting little resistance, quickly conquers the island.

AUGUST 12 — An armistice ends hostilities in the Spanish-American War. A definitive peace treaty is signed by President McKinley on February 10, 1899, in which the United States acquires Puerto Rico and Guam, and Spain gives up Cuba. The United States also agrees to purchase certain Spanish holdings in the Philippines for $20 million; however, most politicians simply interpret this as the purchase of all the Philippine islands.

1899

MAVERICK UNIVERSITY OF CHICAGO economist Thorstein Veblen publishes *The Theory of the Leisure Class,* a brilliant, good-humored, and highly provocative assault on America's moneyed elite. The book slowly but surely gains a wide readership throughout the nation.

SCOTT JOPLIN, an African-American pianist and composer from Sedalia, Missouri, publishes the "Maple Leaf Rag," ushering in the era of ragtime.

1899–1901

THE UNITED STATES participates in an international coalition to counter the Boxer Rebellion, an armed insurrection against the European diplomatic and trade community in China. The Boxers (as the insurgents are called) are crushed, and China is forced by the Boxer Protocol of September 7, 1901, to pay the European powers and the United States a large indemnity, to open trade fully to the West, and to allow the stationing of American and European troops in China to ensure the security of these nations' interests in the country.

1899–1902

A LARGE FILIPINO faction led by Emilio Aguinaldo refuses to acknowledge U.S. sovereignty over the Philippines and, on January 20, 1899, declares independence. The U.S. counters this "Philippine Insurrection" by sending some 70,000 troops. By May 6, 1902, this force suppresses the insurrection, but it does not succeed in crushing the independence movement.

1900

SEPTEMBER 8 — A hurricane roars across Galveston Island, Texas, submerging the city of Galveston beneath the waters of the Gulf of Mexico. Of the 37,789 people living in Galveston at the time, 6,000 to

10,000 are killed and another 6,000 badly injured. The combination of 120-mile-per-hour winds and 20-foot floodwaters rips 3,636 homes from their foundations. Although it remains the single deadliest natural disaster in American history, Hurricane Katrina in 2005 will affect more people and, in monetary terms, be far more costly.

NOVEMBER 6 — William McKinley is reelected president, once again defeating William Jennings Bryan.

1901

THE FIRST LAW TO LIMIT vehicle operating speed is passed. Connecticut imposes a speed limit of 10 miles per hour in cities, 15 mph in villages, and 20 mph in rural areas.

MARCH 2 — Congress adopts the Platt Amendment, which conditions the withdrawal of American troops occupying the new republic of Cuba on the inclusion of clauses in the Cuban constitution that effectively make Cuba a client of the United States.

MARCH 12 — Steel magnate–turned–philanthropist Andrew Carnegie endows the New York Public Library. Carnegie's $5.2 million gift funds a main library and 39 branches throughout the city.

MAY 27 — The Supreme Court decides the so-called Insular Cases, holding that Puerto Rico, the Philippines, Guam, and Hawaii—all newly acquired island (hence "insular") possessions—are neither foreign countries nor part of the United States. The court effectively answers the question "Does the Constitution follow the flag?" by establishing a special framework for the application of the Constitution to these islands, a framework that does not automatically extend full constitutional rights to all areas under American control.

SEPTEMBER 2 — A remark by Vice President Theodore Roosevelt expresses his personal political philosophy using a phrase borrowed from a West African proverb: "Speak softly and carry a big stick." During Roosevelt's presidency, the "big stick" is to become part and parcel of American foreign policy.

SEPTEMBER 6 — President William McKinley is shot at point-blank range by an anarchist, Leon Czolgosz, at the Pan-American Exposition in Buffalo, New York. McKinley dies on September 14, and Vice President Theodore Roosevelt assumes office.

1902

JANUARY 24 — A treaty purchasing some of the Virgin Islands from Denmark is signed. The consummation of the purchase is delayed until January 17, 1917, after Denmark ratifies a revised treaty of August 14, 1916.

1903

HENRY JAMES, an American novelist living in London, publishes *The Ambassadors,* an elaborately nuanced novel that highlights the differences between the American and European character. With this rarified masterpiece, the American novel reaches a lofty height of intellectual sophistication.

JACK LONDON PUBLISHES *The Call of the Wild,* which blends London's experiences as a Klondike gold prospector with his ideas about nature, the wilderness, civilization, the power of instinct and ancestral memory, and the struggle for existence. Between this elemental novel and James's rarified *The Ambassadors* is contained the enormous range of American literature at the turn of the new century.

FILMMAKER EDWIN S. PORTER, working for the Edison Company, directs the first true narrative motion picture, *The Great Train Robbery,* which launches the medium of film as a major form of mass entertainment and sets the United States on a course to become the primary source of the world's movies. (The seemingly inexhaustible Thomas A. Edison had developed the Kinetograph—a motion picture camera—and a peep-hole motion picture viewer called the Kinetoscope beginning in 1888. His company started producing motion pictures in 1892 and began commercial theatrical exhibition of the films in 1896.)

MACHINIST AND ENGINEER HENRY FORD founds the Ford Motor Company to manufacture automobiles.

U.S. POPULATION: 75,995,000

JANUARY 22 — The Hay-Herrán Treaty, signed with Colombia, secures a 99-year lease and sovereignty over a "Canal Zone," through which the Panama Canal is to be dug. After the Colombian senate rejects the treaty, the Roosevelt administration supports a revolution that makes Panama independent of Colombia. On November 18, the Hay-Bunau-Varilla Treaty is negotiated with Panama to give the United States permanent sovereignty over the Canal Zone.

FEBRUARY 14 — A cabinet-level U.S. Department of Commerce and Labor is created by Congress.

MARCH 10 — President Roosevelt invokes the Sherman Antitrust Act to prosecute the monopolistic practices of the Northern Securities Company, a J. P. Morgan firm. During his presidency, the aggressively antitrust Roosevelt earns the title of "trust buster."

OCTOBER 1–OCTOBER 13 — The first World Series of base-ball is played, pitting the Pittsburgh Pirates against the Boston Red Sox (then called the Bostons or Boston Ball Club). Boston takes the Series, five games to three.

DECEMBER 17 — At Kill Devil Hill, Kitty Hawk, North Carolina, Orville Wright flies a 750-pound aircraft he and his brother Wilbur designed and built in their Dayton, Ohio, bicycle shop. A 12-horsepower gasoline engine (also of their own design) propels the airplane for 12 seconds a few feet above the ground over a distance of 120 feet. It is the first manned flight by a heavier-than-air craft.

1904

JOURNALIST IDA TARBELL publishes *The History of the Standard Oil Company,* a sensational exposé of John D. Rockefeller's gargantuan vertical monopoly. The book inaugurates the era of the "muckraker," a word Theodore Roosevelt borrows from *Pilgrim's Progress,* the 17th-century allegory by John Bunyan that is still very familiar to early 20th-century American school-children and adults alike. One of Bunyan's characters refuses to look up to heaven because he is obsessed with raking the muck (an allegorical representation of immorality and corruption) below. The early 20th-century muckrakers immerse themselves in the corruption of American society in order to expose it and, ultimately, to bring about reform.

NOVEMBER 8 — Theodore Roosevelt is reelected president, defeating Democrat Alton B. Parker.

1905

JULY 7 — "Big Bill" Haywood founds the International Workers of the World (IWW) in Chicago as an alternative to the more conservative American Federation of Labor. Whereas the AFL cultivates the membership of skilled workers, the IWW recruits unskilled labor. The radical organization provokes a mixture of contempt and fear in mainstream America, which calls IWW members

"Wobblies" and says the organization's initials stand for "I Won't Work."

AUGUST 9 — President Roosevelt mediates an end to the bloody Russo-Japanese War by convening a peace conference between the belligerents at Portsmouth, New Hampshire, which yields the Treaty of Portsmouth on September 5.

1906

UPTON SINCLAIR publishes *The Jungle,* a novel set in the stockyards of Chicago and exposing, in vividly nauseating detail, the sordid practices of the meatpacking industry, which greedily purveys tainted meat to the American masses. The novel is not only a muckraking classic but also presents the meatpackers as a melodramatic metaphor for the worst of American big business: a heartless monolith willing to sicken or even kill the public for the sake of profit. The novel electrifies the nation and moves Congress to pass the Pure Food and Drug Act and Meat Inspection Act.

APRIL 7 — American electrical engineer Lee De Forest, inventor of the triode tube (which becomes a primary component of modern radios and most other electronic equipment before the introduction of transistors), makes a spectacular 40,000-watt trans-Atlantic wireless broadcast from New York to Ireland. Although the Irish-Italian inventor Guglielmo Marconi had already made a trans-Atlantic transmission in 1901, De Forest's powerful triode-based system is the birth of modern radio technology and transforms wireless into a truly practical medium.

APRIL 18 — A devastating earthquake hits San Francisco, igniting fires that sweep the city for three days. Nearly 500 city blocks are leveled or burned down and an estimated 25,000 buildings destroyed. Only 478 deaths are reported, but modern authorities believe this a deliberate underestimate prompted by powerful real estate interests; the quake and fires probably kill more than 3,000.

JUNE 30 — Congress passes the Pure Food and Drug Act and, with it, the Meat Inspection Act. The Pure Food and Drug Act bars the sale of adulterated foods and drugs and prohibits dishonest, exaggerated, or fraudulent claims on product labels. The Meat Inspection Act sets sanitary standards for meatpackers and requires federal inspection to confirm compliance.

DECEMBER 10 — President Roosevelt is awarded the Nobel Peace Prize for his role in ending the Russo-Japanese War. He is the first American winner of the prize.

DECEMBER 12 — President Roosevelt appoints Oscar S. Straus secretary of commerce and labor. Straus is the first Jew appointed to a presidential cabinet.

1907

PHILOSOPHER AND PSYCHOLOGIST William James publishes *Pragmatism: A New Name for Old Ways of Thinking,* which proposes that the meaning as well as the truth of any idea is a function of its practical outcome. Born of an American culture of action and enterprise, the philosophy in turn exerts a great intellectual influence on subsequent American thought and American ethics.

FEBRUARY 24 — President Roosevelt concludes the "Gentlemen's Agreement" with Japanese representatives, by which Japan agrees to deny passports to laborers intending to enter the United States and recognizes the U.S. right to exclude Japanese immigrants holding passports originally issued for other countries. The agreement reflects continuing anti-Asian racial antagonism in the United States, exemplified in the formation (in 1905) of a Japanese and Korean Exclusion League and the segregation of Asian children in the San Francisco school system. The Gentlemen's Agreement ends school segregation in San Francisco but bolsters the Immigration Act of 1907, signed by Roosevelt on February 20, restricting the immigration of Japanese laborers.

1908

OCTOBER 1 — Henry Ford introduces his Model T. Priced at $850 upon its introduction, it is much cheaper than other automobiles of the period, but still beyond the reach of the masses. Ford's perfection of assembly-line mass production enables him to reduce the price to $368 by 1916, making the Model T affordable by those earning an average wage. By the last year of production, 1927, Ford has turned out 15 million Model Ts, which transform not only the landscape by spurring the building of roads and the development of suburbs but also American culture, by providing greater freedom and stimulating an ethic of consumerism. The effect on the American workplace is mixed: Ford provides a good wage to semiskilled and even unskilled workers, but the assembly line creates a soul-killing work environment demanding monotonous, anonymous, alienating labor that shackles human beings to machines.

NOVEMBER 3 — William Howard Taft is elected president, defeating perennial Democratic candidate William Jennings Bryan. Handpicked by Theodore Roosevelt as his successor, Taft's conservative politics and policies soon disappoint the dynamic Roosevelt.

DECEMBER 26 — African-American boxer Jack Johnson takes the world heavyweight boxing crown from Tommy Burns in 14 rounds fought in Sydney, Australia. Johnson emerges as the nation's first black sports hero.

1909

THE AFRICAN-AMERICAN SOCIOLOGIST W. E. B. Du Bois and a group of black and white activists led by Oswald Garrison Villard, grandson of the abolitionist William Lloyd Garrison, found the National Association for the Advancement of Colored People (NAACP), which emerges as the nation's leading advocacy group for African Americans.

BELGIAN-BORN AMERICAN CHEMIST Leo H. Baekeland invents a synthetic thermosetting resin he calls Bakelite, the most important precursor of modern plastic.

FEBRUARY 21 — Adm. George Dewey completes a worldwide tour leading the U.S. Navy's "Great White Fleet," an intimidating demonstration of American naval might.

APRIL 6 — Naval officer Robert E. Peary and his African-American valet and fellow explorer, Matthew Alexander Henson, accompanied by four Eskimos, become the first men to reach the North Pole.

1910

MAY 16 — The U.S. Bureau of Mines is established as part of the Department of the Interior. The bureau regulates the operation of mines, particularly with regard to issues of safety.

JUNE 25 — Congress passes the Mann Act, prohibiting the interstate or international transportation of women "for immoral purposes." The act grows out of intense nation-wide concern over "white slavery."

AUGUST 31 — Disappointed by the conservatism of President William Howard Taft, his handpicked successor, Theodore Roosevelt delivers his "New Nationalism" speech at Osawatomie, New York, setting out what he calls the "Square Deal for Americans." It is a progressive political program calling for a graduated income tax, government regulation of monopolies and trusts, protection for the rights of labor, conservation of the natural environment, and a strong army and navy. For the most part, this liberal program becomes the platform of 1912 Democratic presidential candidate Woodrow Wilson and serves as the foundation for liberal politics throughout the 20th century.

1911

FREDERICK TAYLOR, a former steel plant foreman, publishes *Principles of Scientific Management,* a rigorous system for rationalizing the human element in industrial production. "Taylorism," which soon sweeps American industry, calls for idiosyncrasy and "outmoded" individuality of craftsmanship to be replaced by strict management control of all work procedures and production methods so that the pace of production is never tied to any particular worker or set of workers. While Taylorism increases productivity, it also creates great dissatisfaction among workers, who feel increasingly dehumanized, exploited, and alienated.

JANUARY 21 — Wisconsin senator Robert M. La Follette founds the National Progressive Republican League. The organization promotes progressive legislation, including direct primaries, direct election of delegates to national political conventions, and amendments to state constitutions that provide for popular initiative, referendum, and recall. Many consider La Follette's populism excessively radical.

MARCH 25 — A fire breaks out at the Triangle Shirtwaist Company, a Manhattan garment sweatshop. The building, overcrowded with mostly immigrant workers, is—like many other urban workshops—a firetrap. It has a single fire escape, and its emergency exit doors are locked, blocked, or inoperative. Of more than 500 employees, 146 are killed, many leaping to their deaths in a frenzied effort to escape the flames. Most of the victims are young women. The tragedy draws national attention to the evils of sweatshop conditions and also motivates municipalities to revise building and fire codes. National and state labor laws are also reformed.

1912

AFRICAN-AMERICAN educator, diplomat, and poet James Weldon Johnson anonymously publishes *Autobiography of an Ex-Colored Man,* the fictional memoir of a man of interracial parentage who struggles to seek his identity in racist America. Slow to gain recognition, the novel ultimately emerges as a seminal work of African-American literature and as a penetrating exploration of the role race plays in the collective American psyche.

APRIL 14–15 — During the night, the British liner *Titanic* strikes an iceberg and sinks with loss of some 1,500 lives, including those of several prominent Americans. Many view the sinking of this brand-new "unsinkable" wonder ship as a hard lesson in the limits of modern technology.

NOVEMBER 5 — Democrat Woodrow Wilson, reformist governor of New Jersey and former president of Princeton University, is elected president, having run on a platform of idealistic progressive reform. This election sees the emergence of highly influential third parties, which appeal to voters who feel poorly served by both the Democrats and the Republicans. The most important are the Socialist Party, which runs labor leader Eugene V. Debs as its candidate, and the Progressive (or Bull Moose) Party, which nominates Theodore Roosevelt. Roosevelt outpolls Republican William Howard Taft (88 electoral votes to 8), but loses to Democrat Woodrow Wilson (435).

1913

FEBRUARY 25 — Congress adopts the 16th Amendment, providing for a federal income tax to be levied on individuals and businesses. The vast majority of the American people support the amendment, believing that a tax pegged to income will oblige the wealthy to "pay their fair share."

MAY 14 — Mega-industrialist John D. Rockefeller performs the largest single philanthropic act in history by creating the Rockefeller Foundation, which he endows to the tune of $100,000,000.

MAY 19 — California governor Hiram W. Johnson signs the Webb Alien Land-Holding Bill, which bars Japanese

U.S. POPULATION: 91,972,266

nationals from owning land in California. The bill is passed and signed over protests from President Wilson and the Japanese government.

MAY 31 — The 17th Amendment goes into effect, providing for the popular election of U.S. senators. Prior to this amendment, senators were chosen by the legislatures of each state.

OCTOBER 10 — The Panama Canal is completed when President Wilson presses a button in the White House, which touches off an explosion in Panama, blowing up the Gamboa Dike and thereby joining the waters of the Pacific with those of the Atlantic.

1914

W. C. HANDY, a black bandleader and composer, unable to find a white publisher for his "St. Louis Blues," publishes the song himself, not only creating the first important African-American-owned music publishing company but also nationalizing and popularizing the uniquely American musical styles of blues and jazz.

APRIL 21 — After the Mexican government of Victoriano Huerta arrests several U.S. Marines in Tampico, Mexico, President Wilson orders an amphibious invasion of Veracruz with the purpose of blocking German arms shipments to Huerta and securing an apology for the arrest of the marines. In the face of the invasion, Huerta backs down, resigning the presidency on July 15. The

Veracruz occupation ends on November 23 without further incident.

MAY 7 — Congress votes a resolution establishing a national Mother's Day.

JUNE 28 — World War I is triggered in Europe by the assassination of the Austrian archduke Franz Ferdinand and his wife, the Grand Duchess Sophie, in the obscure Balkan capital of Sarajevo. As the war rapidly enlarges, President Wilson firmly declares U.S. neutrality on August 4.

DECEMBER 8 — Irving Berlin's first musical, *Watch Your Step*, opens in New York City. Berlin eventually becomes one of America's most popular, prolific, and influential songwriters.

1915

JANUARY 25 — Alexander Graham Bell, the inventor of the telephone, makes the first transcontinental telephone call to Thomas A. Watson, the same man he had called on the very first telephone 39 years earlier, on March 10, 1876.

JANUARY 28 — Congress establishes the U.S. Coast Guard.

MAY 7 — The British liner *Lusitania* is torpedoed and sunk by a German U-boat, with the loss of American passengers' lives. The attack outrages the American people and begins to turn U.S. public and political opinion against Germany.

JUNE 7 — William Jennings Bryan, secretary of state in the cabinet of Woodrow Wilson, resigns to protest what he considers Wilson's alarming drift toward war.

SUMMER–GEORGE CRAM COOK leads a group of writers and artists in the creation of the Provincetown Players in Massachusetts. The company quickly emerges as the nation's most exciting and innovative theater group. In 1916, it is the first to produce a play by the figure who will be generally acknowledged as America's most important playwright, Eugene O'Neill, staging his *Bound East for Cardiff.*

DECEMBER 4 — The Ku Klux Klan, founded after the Civil War but dormant by the end of the Reconstruction era, is revived in Georgia when the state grants it a corporate charter. Within a few years, Klansmen begin terrorizing blacks throughout the South.

DECEMBER 4 — Henry Ford and a group of prominent pacifists set off for Europe aboard the *Peace Ship,* an ocean liner Ford has chartered. Ford believes he can talk all sides into laying down their arms. Though noble, the voyage proves futile.

1916

CARL SANDBURG PUBLISHES *Chicago Poems,* a popular work that signals a break with genteel American poetic traditions.

PHILOSOPHER AND EDUCATOR John Dewey publishes *Democracy and Education,* in which he advances his conception of democracy not just as a form of government but also as a mode of social organization. Democracy, Dewey argues, furnishes an environment in which the individual may enlarge his or her own experience and in which society, collectively, may expand its intellectual and ethical horizons. To maximize democratic opportunity, Dewey proposes an innovative system of "progressive education."

BRIG. GEN. JOHN TALIAFERO THOMPSON invents the Thompson submachine ("Tommy") gun, a light, powerful automatic weapon. The U.S. military adopts it, but the gun becomes most famous in the 1920s and 1930s as the American gangster's weapon of choice.

JANUARY 28 — President Wilson names Louis D. Brandeis to the Supreme Court. He is the first Jew to hold the office of Supreme Court justice.

MARCH 9 — The violence of revolution-racked Mexico spills across the border into the United States when revolutionary and bandit Pancho Villa leads a raid against Columbus, New Mexico, in which 10 American civilians and 14 U.S. soldiers are killed. In response, President Wilson orders Maj. Gen. John J. Pershing to lead a "Punitive Expedition" to capture or kill Villa and his men. Some 15,000 U.S. troops invade Mexico on March 14, but fail to find Villa—though they do locate and kill most of his chief lieutenants and prevent any further raids. The Punitive Expedition ends on February 5, 1917.

OCTOBER 16 — Birth-control and sex-education activist Margaret Sanger and others open the nation's first birth control clinic, in Brooklyn.

NOVEMBER 7 — Woodrow Wilson is reelected president by a narrow margin over Republican Charles Evans Hughes. Wilson's victory is in large measure due to his campaign slogan: "He kept us out of war!"

1917–1918

THE UNITED STATES fights in World War I.

1917

TWO STARS OF THE FLEDGLING medium of motion pictures strike it big. Charlie Chaplin, the nation's premier film comic actor, signs an 18-film contract with First National Pictures for $1 million, and Mary Pickford, dubbed "America's sweetheart," becomes the first woman in America to earn a million dollars in a single year. Their sensational success presages an American celebrity culture created almost exclusively by the motion picture industry.

FEBRUARY 24 — British authorities hand U.S. ambassador Walter Hines Page the "Zimmermann Note," an intercepted telegram from German foreign minister Alfred Zimmermann to the German ambassador in Mexico instructing the ambassador to propose a German-Mexican military alliance against the United States. Germany promises to help Mexico regain the territories it lost in the

Mexican War. President Wilson makes the note public on March 1, and it becomes part of the basis on which he later asks Congress for a declaration of war against Germany.

APRIL 2 — Jeannette Rankin, a Republican from Montana, is seated as the first U.S. congresswoman. (In 1948, Margaret Chase Smith of Maine will become the first female senator, having earlier served in the House.)

APRIL 2 — President Wilson asks Congress for a declaration of war against Germany. The Senate votes for war, 82 to 6, on April 4; the House votes in favor on April 6, 373 to 50 (among those opposed is newly seated Jeannette Rankin). Wilson signs the declaration on April 6.

MAY 18 — Congress passes the Selective Service Act, authorizing conscription of men into the armed forces for the first time since the Civil War. By the time the war ends in November 1918, the U.S. Army swells from 133,000 officers and men (1914) to 4.5 million.

JUNE 15 — Congress passes the Espionage Act. The most repressive legislation since the Alien and Sedition Acts of 1798, the act makes it a federal crime to obstruct military recruitment, foster "disloyalty" in the armed forces, or engage in any other disloyal activity, action, or speech.

1918

MAY 15 — The nation's first airmail service begins, between New York and Washington.

JUNE 4 — In the Battle of Château-Thierry, the first major engagement of World War I in which the U.S. Army plays a central role, the U.S. Second Division halts German forces attempting to advance on Paris.

JUNE 6–25 — The U.S. Marine Corps scores a costly triumph at the Battle of Belleau Wood, which is instrumental in breaking the back of a major German offensive.

JULY 18–August 6 — More than a quarter million U.S. troops participate in the Aisne-Marne Offensive, forcing the Germans to retreat from the Soissons-Reims salient (a strong offensive position bulging into Allied lines) and allowing the Allies to seize the initiative in this crucial phase of World War I.

SEPTEMBER 12–13 — U.S. forces conduct an offensive against the St. Mihiel salient, which the Germans have maintained since the first year of the war. Some of the Germans are driven out but the retreat of others is cut off, so that 15,000 prisoners of war are taken.

SEPTEMBER 14 — Socialist and labor leader Eugene V. Debs is sentenced to ten years' imprisonment for violating the Espionage Act. The sentence outrages liberal elements throughout the United States. Debs is released in 1921.

SEPTEMBER 26–NOVEMBER 11 — The United States fights its biggest campaign of the war, sending 1.2 million troops against the Germans in the Meuse-Argonne Offensive. U.S. forces succeed in cutting off the Germans' principal supply line, the Sedan-Mézières railroad.

NOVEMBER 11 — An armistice ends the Great War at 11 a.m.—the 11th hour of the 11th day of the 11th month.

1918–1919

AN INFLUENZA EPIDEMIC begins during the final year of the war and reaches worldwide pandemic proportions by October 1918, killing 20–40 million worldwide. In the United States, about half a million die.

1919

JANUARY 18 — The Paris Peace Conference, called to conclude World War I, begins. President Wilson is determined to bring about a peace that will include the founding of a League of Nations, an international organization dedicated to the peaceful resolution of disputes among nations. His pledge to the American people and to the world is that the Great War shall be "the war to end wars."

JOHN B. WATSON publishes *Psychology from the Standpoint of a Behaviorist,* laying the foundation of the new field of behaviorist psychology, which reduces human acts and interaction to systems of stimulus and response. The theory suggests that behavior may be deliberately modified, shaped, and manipulated by administering the appropriate stimuli and reinforcement. This approach opens new vistas in psychology, but many criticize it as both inhuman and inhumane.

JANUARY 16 — The 18th Amendment is ratified, outlawing the manufacture, importation, sale, and consumption of alcoholic beverages. The Prohibition Era begins and transforms America into a nation of lawbreakers, as people routinely buy (or even make) and consume illegal beer, wine, and liquor. An underground economy triggers an explosive rise in organized crime.

AUGUST 31 — The Communist Labor Party is organized in Chicago. Part of an international communist movement that has followed the Bolshevik Revolution in Russia, it creates a "Red Scare" throughout the United States, which brings a repressive official response to all manifestations of political dissidence.

AUTUMN — The Treaty of Versailles and the League of Nations meet with resistance from the U.S. Senate, and President Wilson undertakes an exhausting speaking tour of the United States in September, determined to bring the case for the treaty and the league directly to the people. Near the end of the tour, he collapses from exhaustion, then suffers a stroke, which leaves him a semi-invalid for the rest of his second term. (He conducts most public business through his wife, Edith Bolling Wilson.) On November 19, the Senate rejects the Treaty of Versailles 53 to 38 and, with it, the League of Nations. A second vote, in March 1920, also results in defeat for the treaty and the league.

1920

GENERAL MOTORS VICE-PRESIDENT (later, chairman) Alfred P. Sloan, Jr., introduces a new concept in the marketing of technological goods: planned obsolescence. With the automobile market stagnant by the end of the 1910s and the pace of genuine technological innovation insufficiently rapid to grow the market, Sloan proposes a program of annual stylistic alterations, which he believes will give consumers the feeling that the automobile they own is obsolete and therefore will motivate the purchase of a new model. Planned obsolescence does stimulate the market, but also diverts corporate research and development from significant technological innovation to mere cosmetic changes. By the 1970s, American automakers will find their products eclipsed by more technologically advanced imports from Japan.

JANUARY 2 — U.S. Attorney General A. Mitchell Palmer authorizes federal agents to round up suspected communist sympathizers in massive raids carried out in 33 cities on a single evening. A total of 6,000 persons, including American citizens and recent immigrants, are arrested. Ultimately, 556 of those arrested are deported, but other convictions and deportation orders are overturned, and Palmer himself is discredited. Palmer's protégé, a young Justice Department zealot named J. Edgar Hoover, escapes censure and goes on to lead what will become the Federal Bureau of Investigation (FBI).

APRIL 15 — Frank Parmenter and Alesandro Berardelli, the paymaster and a guard at a South Braintree, Massachusetts, shoe factory, are killed during an armed robbery. Three weeks later, Nicola Sacco and Bartolomeo Vanzetti, workingmen and self-proclaimed anarchists, are arrested and accused of the crime. Despite much exculpatory evidence, the immigrant anarchists are convicted. Their case becomes the greatest cause célèbre of the decade; from all over the world, famous authors, jurists, political leaders, and religious leaders (including the pope) protest the convictions and the sentence of death. The case is repeatedly appealed, the conviction upheld, and pleas for clemency denied. Sacco and Vanzetti are executed on August 23, 1927—victims, as many see it, of their political convictions and their foreign birth.

AUGUST 24 — Tennessee becomes the 36th of the 48 states to ratify the 19th Amendment giving American women the right to vote in all elections.

NOVEMBER 2 — Warren G. Harding is elected president, defeating Democrat James M. Cox by a landslide: 16,152,200 to 9,147,353. Women, voting for the first time in national elections, had been expected to favor the liberal Democrat, but, in fact, they vote in large numbers for Harding, who promises "a return to normalcy"—meaning a retreat from Wilsonian idealism and its engagement with international politics. Harding is the product of the so-called smoke-filled room, a closed-door caucus. An affable party hack, he does whatever his Republican handlers tell him to do, and he presides over the most corrupt presidential administration since that of Ulysses S. Grant.

NOVEMBER 2 — Pittsburgh's radio station KDKA broadcasts election results on the very night that the polls close. This is generally regarded as the nation's first commercial radio broadcast.

1921

THE AFRICAN-AMERICAN agricultural scientist George Washington Carver appears before Congress to present the many uses of the peanut—among them peanut butter (which he has invented)—and the sweet potato. In his long career, Carver develops peanut- and sweet potato–based lubricants, plastic products, dyes, pharmaceuticals, inks, wood stains, and cosmetics, as well as tapioca and molasses substitutes. Carver's work not only creates a host of new American industries but also rescues many Southern farmers, black and white, from the economic instability and outright poverty born of exclusive reliance on cotton (though Carver also creates the highly successful "Carver's Hybrid," a sturdy cross between short- and long-stalk cotton).

MAY 19 — President Harding signs the nation's first generally restrictive immigration act. It introduces a quota sys-

U.S. POPULATION: 105,710,620

tem that restricts immigration to 3 percent of the number of each nationality reported in the Census of 1910. Total immigration is capped at 357,000 persons annually. The legislation is a symptom of the acute xenophobia that prevails during the Harding years.

1922

T. S. ELIOT, an American poet living in London, publishes *The Waste Land,* a long, richly symbolic poem that captures the spiritual malaise of postwar Western civilization and creates a literary sensation.

1923

AUGUST 2 — President Harding dies in San Francisco on his way back from a tour of the West and Alaska. The cause is an embolism, diagnosed as a complication of ptomaine poisoning and pneumonia, but some believe that the president has been poisoned, perhaps by his wife. Harding's administration has been plagued by extensive corruption, including the infamous Teapot Dome Scandal (which comes to a head on June 30, 1924), and he himself has been implicated in extramarital affairs. Vice President Calvin Coolidge becomes president on August 3. "Silent Cal," a tight-lipped Vermonter, continues Harding's policy of "normalcy" and isolationism, but does act effectively against corrupt elements in the administration and earns unexpected popularity.

SEPTEMBER 15 — Oklahoma governor John Calloway Walton puts his state under martial law to combat the rampant terrorism of the Ku Klux Klan. The exposure of KKK misdeeds begins to turn national public opinion against the Klan.

NOVEMBER 6 — Jacob Schick secures a patent for the world's first electric razor, which he begins manufacturing in 1931.

1924

THOMAS WATSON, president of CTR (the Computing Tabulating Recording Company), a maker of tabulating machines for government and business, renames the firm IBM (International Business Machines). Under Watson's leadership, IBM becomes the world's leading maker of innovative electromechanical calculating devices, collation and sorting machines, typewriters, and other machines for business. IBM joins forces with an electrical engineering team from Harvard University to develop the Mark I in 1940, generally considered the first modern programmable computer. An electromechanical device, the Mark I is used extensively by the military during World War II and is the precursor of ENIAC, the first all-electronic computer, unveiled by University of Pennsylvania engineers in 1946.

JUNE 30 — A federal grand jury indicts Albert B. Fall, former secretary of the interior; Harry Sinclair, president of Mammoth Oil; and Edward Doheny, president of Pan-American Oil and Transport, for bribery and conspiracy to defraud the United States. Sinclair is accused of having bribed Fall to obtain a lease for the Teapot Dome federal oil reserve in Wyoming—a strategic oil reserve intended exclusively to supply the U.S. Navy with fuel oil for its warships. Doheny is similarly charged with regard to leases on the Elk Hills naval reserves in California. The Teapot Dome Scandal is the most serious of the multiple scandals that have characterized the Harding administration, and its exposure makes many Americans supremely cynical about the integrity of their government.

JULY 21 — Nathan Leopold and Richard Loeb, two privileged Chicago youths and students at the University of Chicago, receive life sentences for the "thrill murder" of a boy, Bobby Franks. The act was apparently motivated by Leopold and Loeb's desire to commit the perfect crime—horrible, random, and unsolvable. Clarence Darrow, America's most famous defense attorney, defended the pair, not to plead their innocence (there is no doubt as to their guilt) but to save them from the death penalty, which Darrow opposes even as punishment for the most horrific crimes. For the first time in legal history, a lawyer pleaded that his clients were psychopaths, not insane but constitutionally incapable of distinguishing right from wrong. On this basis he wins life sentences.

NOVEMBER 4 — Bland and colorless, Calvin Coolidge is just what the electorate wants in 1924, and he is reelected in a landslide over Democrat John W. Davis and a host of third-party contenders, including Progressive Robert M. La Follette.

NOVEMBER 30 — RCA (the Radio Corporation of America) transmits photographs via radio from London to New York City. The technology presages both facsimile and television transmission.

1925

F. SCOTT FITZGERALD, a glamorous rising literary star, publishes his masterpiece, *The Great Gatsby,* an incisive and lyrical exploration of the Roaring Twenties, romantic love, and the American dream as well as its corruption. The novel is not a popular success, but it comes to be recognized, well after Fitzgerald's death, as a monument of American literature.

THEODORE DREISER, already famed as the greatest exponent of realistic naturalism in American literature, publishes *An American Tragedy,* an ambitious work based on an actual murder in upstate New York. The novel explores the motives behind human action, compounded by social values, animal urges, and genetically influenced destiny. Many consider *the* book the Great American Novel.

JULY 10–21 — The so-called Scopes Monkey Trial takes place in Dayton, Tennessee, and rivets the nation. High school teacher John T. Scopes is tried for having violated Tennessee state law by teaching Darwin's theory of evolution in his biology class. Seeing his prosecution as an attack on free speech, the American Civil Liberties Union (ACLU) hires Clarence Darrow to defend Scopes. The prosecution is fronted by William Jennings Bryan, perennial populist presidential candidate and a Christian fundamentalist with a reputation as a great orator. In the end, it is Bryan's fundamentalism that is put on public trial. Scopes is convicted, but fined a token sum of $100. Humiliated before the nation, Bryan dies on July 26. The debate over evolution versus "creationism" in the classroom has yet to be put to rest.

AUGUST 8 — A Ku Klux Klan rally draws 40,000 KKK members in a march through the streets of Washington, D.C.

DECEMBER 17 — Army Air Corps officer Billy Mitchell, a passionate advocate for the development of airpower as the key component of American military might, is found guilty of insubordination by a court-martial and is suspended from the army for 5 years. He has publicly criticized the army and navy for "incompetency, criminal negligence, and almost treasonable administration of national defense" in (according to Mitchell) ignoring the safe and progressive development of airpower. In response to the verdict, Mitchell resigns and continues his airpower campaign as a private citizen. Although he dies in 1936 before it begins, World War II vindicates his views, and he is today considered one of the intellectual and doctrinal founders of the modern U.S. Air Force.

1926

HENRY FORD replaces the nationally prevailing 60-hour workweek with the 40-hour week in his auto plants. Most manufacturers follow suit, and this becomes the model throughout the United States, subsequently embodied in federal labor law.

APRIL — The Book-of-the-Month Club is founded, providing a powerful new means of marketing books to the masses and forming popular literary taste.

MAY 9 — Rear Adm. Richard Byrd and aviator Floyd Bennett make the first successful flight over the North Pole.

MAY 10 — U.S. Marines land in Nicaragua to put down an uprising led by leftist Augusto César Sandino against Emiliano Chamorro, a pro-U.S. conservative army chief who had seized the government the year before. This marks the beginning of periodic U.S. involvement in Nicaraguan affairs (which will extend into the 1980s), its support of repressive right-wing leaders, and its opposition to the left-wing Sandino and his followers, called Sandinistas. Sandino is killed in 1934 after eight years of guerrilla warfare.

AUGUST 5 — *Don Juan,* starring John Barrymore, is the first commercial "talking picture" shown to an audience. The movie employs phonographically recorded sound rather than a sound track integral to the physical film. The first full-length "talkie," featuring both music and dialogue fully synchronized with the visual action (although still recorded on disk), is *The Jazz Singer,* starring Al Jolson, which premieres on October 6, 1927.

AUGUST 6 — New Yorker Gertrude Ederle becomes the first woman to swim the English Channel; she swims 14 hours, 31 minutes.

1927

APRIL 7 — Television is first publicly demonstrated when Walter S. Gifford, president of the American Telephone and Telegraph Company (AT&T), speaks via video link from New York City to Secretary of Commerce Herbert Hoover in Washington.

MAY 20 — Charles A. Lindbergh, a tall, handsome, modest 25-year-old aviator, takes off from Roosevelt Field, Long Island, and begins a flight across the Atlantic Ocean. He lands 33.5 hours later at Le Bourget Field outside of Paris, becoming the first person to fly solo from America to Europe. Lindbergh becomes an international celebrity and his feat does much to advance the development and acceptance of commercial passenger aviation.

AUGUST 10 — The Mount Rushmore memorial is dedicated. The work of sculptor Gutzon Borglum and a large crew, the sculpture features the busts of George Washington, Thomas Jefferson, Abraham Lincoln, and Theodore Roosevelt blasted from the side of the South Dakota mountain to a height of 500 feet. The work is visible for some 60 miles.

NOVEMBER 13 — The Holland Tunnel, the nation's first underwater motor vehicle tunnel, connecting Manhattan with Jersey City, New Jersey, is completed.

1928

JUNE 17 — Amelia Earhart captures the world's imagination by becoming the first woman to make a trans-Atlantic flight, flying from Trepassy Bay, Newfoundland, to Burry Port, Wales, in 20 hours, 40 minutes. She is accompanied by a mechanic and copilot, both men.

AUGUST 27 — The Kellogg-Briand Pact, drawn up by U.S. secretary of state Frank Kellogg and French minister of foreign affairs Aristide Briand, outlaws war. It is signed by the governments of the United States, France, Germany, Belgium, Great Britain, Italy, Japan, and Czechoslovakia, all destined to become principals in World War II.

NOVEMBER 6 — Despite his popularity, Calvin Coolidge declines to run for a second elected term, and Herbert Hoover, the second-choice Republican candidate, is elected, defeating Democrat Alfred E. Smith by a land-slide margin.

1929

FEBRUARY 14 — The "St. Valentine's Day Massacre" is perpetrated by Al "Scarface" Capone, who orders five of his gang to gun down seven members of the rival George "Bugs" Moran gang outside Moran's northside Chicago garage. This outrage finally turns public opinion against Capone and other crime bosses—hitherto seen largely as harmless purveyors of Prohibition-era booze—and brings demands for police action to "clean up" lawless urban America.

MAY 16 — The Academy of Motion Picture Arts and Sciences presents the first Academy Awards. Best picture for 1927–1928 is the spectacular World War I flying epic *Wings,* best actor is Emil Jannings (for performances in *The Way of All Flesh* and *The Last Command*), and best actress is Janet Gaynor (*Seventh Heaven, Street Angel,* and *Sunrise*).

SEPTEMBER 16 — The phrase "banned in Boston," first used in the late 19th century, enters the popular American lexicon when Boston's mayor closes down Eugene O'Neill's Pulitzer Prize–winning play *Strange Interlude,* citing its "obscenity."

OCTOBER 29 — The Great Depression begins on "Black Tuesday" when panic-stricken investors sell a record 16,410,030 shares of stock on the New York Stock Exchange (NYSE) at sacrifice prices. The sell-off continues for the next several days, so that by December 1, NYSE stocks have lost $26 billion of their value. During the booming 1920s, industrial production had soared beyond the financial ability of consumers to purchase what was produced. As demand shrank, workers lost jobs. Because jobless people cannot create demand, production fell even further, creating yet more joblessness. Stocks lost value, and banks failed. The capitalist economic system imploded.

NOVEMBER 29 — U.S. Navy lieutenant commander Richard Byrd, who flew over the North Pole in 1926, flies over the South Pole.

1930

APRIL 22 — In an effort to avoid an arms race, the United States, Great Britain, and Japan sign the London Naval Treaty. Essentially, the treaty mandates parity of naval power among the three powers, specifying tonnage limits for battleships, aircraft carriers, and other warships. Italy and France also participate, but not at the same level.

JULY 3 — President Hoover signs the Veterans Administration Act, creating a single agency to administer benefits for former service personnel.

1931

MARCH 25 — In Scottsboro, Alabama, nine African-American youths, ages 13 to 19, are taken off a freight train, arrested, tried, and, on the shallowest possible evidence, hurriedly convicted of raping two white women riding in the same freight car. All nine of the "Scottsboro Boys" are sentenced to death, and the case becomes a national cause for various liberal groups. The International Labor Defense (ILD), a Communist-backed group, vies with the National Association for the Advancement of Colored People (NAACP) to provide appeal attorneys. The "boys" remain loyal to the ILD lawyers, whose appeal of the convictions fails in the Alabama courts but succeeds in the U.S. Supreme Court on the grounds that the accused were not adequately defended at the original trial. In a new trial, the defendants are again convicted, and again the Supreme Court overturns the convictions, this time on the grounds that the jury was all white. At the time, Alabama law bars blacks from juries, so the Supreme Court decision sparks an eventually successful battle to include blacks on juries. Prosecutors fail to win the third trial (1936) and agree to a plea bargain that releases four defendants but commits the other five to long prison sentences. The state eventually frees or paroles all except one inmate, who escapes in 1948 and is subsequently recaptured and convicted of another crime. The last surviving "Scottsboro boy," Clarence Norris, having fled parole in 1946, is pardoned in 1976.

MAY 1 — The Empire State Building, the world's tallest skyscraper, is dedicated in New York.

1932

MARCH 1 — Twenty-month-old Charles A. Lindbergh, Jr., is abducted from the Hopewell, New Jersey, home of his parents, aviator Charles Lindbergh and author Anne Morrow Lindbergh. The "Lindbergh Kidnapping" becomes a national sensation and is regarded as the "crime of the century." The infant's body is found on May 12 after the payment of a $50,000 ransom. The trial of the only suspect arrested, German immigrant Bruno Richard Hauptmann, begins in January 1935 and ends in February in Flemington, New Jersey. The most celebrated radio and newspaper reporters of the day cover it, H. L. Mencken calling the trial "the greatest story since the Resurrection." On questionable evidence, Hauptmann is convicted of the crime and is executed on April 2, 1936.

MARCH 23 — President Hoover signs the Norris-LaGuardia Anti-Injunction Act, which prohibits the use of injunctions to either maintain anti-union employment contracts or to inhibit strikes and such strike activities as pickets and boycotts. It is a major victory for the rights of labor.

MAY 29 — The "Bonus Army" marches on Washington. By June, some 17,000 unemployed veterans are camped in and around the city. After World War I, Congress had voted veterans of the conflict a "bonus," payable in 1945. Caught in the grip of the Depression, the Bonus Army hopes the march will shame the legislators into releasing the bonus money 13 years early. The House of Representatives votes for immediate payment, but the more conservative Senate opposes it. The marchers riot on July 28, and President Hoover calls out U.S. Army troops, personally led by Chief of Staff Douglas MacArthur. MacArthur successfully disperses the rioters, but deliberately exceeds his orders by raiding a Bonus Army camp (or "Hooverville," as Depression-era shantytowns sheltering the homeless are called) outside the city in Anacostia Flats, Maryland. A fire breaks out in the camp, and two veterans are shot and killed. Most Americans are appalled by the spectacle of the U.S. Army acting against citizens and veterans, and the episode proves politically fatal to Herbert Hoover in an election year.

NOVEMBER 8 — Franklin D. Roosevelt is elected president, defeating Herbert Hoover, who is widely blamed not only for the Great Depression but for failing to take action to provide emergency relief to the legions of poor and unemployed. Campaigning on the pledge of a "New Deal" for America, the charismatic FDR, who radiates optimism though crippled by polio, wins by a landslide: 22,821,857 votes to 15,761,841.

1933

JANUARY–APRIL — With unprecedented energy, FDR sends to Congress a host of sweeping social and economic legislation during the first "Hundred Days" of his presidency.

MARCH 4 — FDR appoints Frances Perkins secretary of labor. She is the first woman appointed to a president's cabinet.

MARCH 5 — In an emergency Sunday session, Congress passes the necessary legislation to implement the weeklong national bank holiday President Roosevelt has declared. Across the country, all banks are closed in order to assess their financial condition and avert runs on the nation's faltering financial institutions.

MARCH 12 — Franklin Roosevelt makes his first presidential "Fireside Chat" to prepare the nation for the reopening of the banks after the bank holiday. While he was New York governor during the late 1920s and early 1930s, FDR had used the new medium of radio to speak informally to citizens of his state. He continues the

U.S. POPULATION: 122,775,046

practice as president, using the radio as a means of entering into the lives of individual families to explain policies for traumatic times, during both the Depression and World War II.

MARCH 31 — At FDR's urging, Congress creates the Civilian Conservation Corps (CCC), employing tens of thousands of jobless young men in nationwide forestry and reforestation projects on public lands.

MAY 12 — Congress passes the Federal Emergency Relief Act, which provides $500 million for direct, emergency relief to desperately poor individuals and families. It is the first time the federal government has directly aided citizens of the United States.

MAY 18 — At FDR's direction, Congress creates the Tennessee Valley Authority (TVA), a vast series of projects to control Tennessee River floods while also harnessing the river for rural electrification.

JUNE 16 — After much debate, Congress passes the National Industrial Recovery Act, introduced by FDR during the Hundred Days. The Act creates both the National Recovery Administration (NRA) as well as the Public Works Administration (PWA). The controversial NRA puts tight controls on industry and business, instituting sweeping reforms in labor practices, including minimum wage restrictions and acceptance of collective bargaining. The PWA puts many thousands to work on public projects, such as road building, construction of schools, and work on other public facilities.

JUNE 16 — Sent to Congress by FDR during the Hundred Days, the Banking Act of 1933 is finally passed. It establishes the Federal Deposit Insurance Corporation (FDIC), by which the federal government insures bank savings accounts to safeguard against failure and thereby restore public confidence in the Depression-beleaguered U.S. banking system.

DECEMBER 5 — Utah becomes the 36th state (of 48) to ratify the 21st Amendment, repealing Prohibition.

DECEMBER 6 — Federal judge John M. Woolsey lifts a federal ban on the importation of Irish novelist James Joyce's masterpiece *Ulysses*. Woolsey overturns the government's assertion that the novel is obscene, and his judicial opinion provides an important aesthetic and intellectual standard by which even morally innovative and daring works of art and literature may be evaluated by weighing their "socially redeeming" values against charges of indecency or obscenity.

1934

MARCH 24 — The Tydings-McDuffie Act is passed, granting independence to the Philippines as of July 4, 1946.

JUNE 28 — The Federal Farm Bankruptcy Act (Frazier-Lemke Act) is signed by President Roosevelt. It declares a moratorium on farm foreclosures during a period in which farm families are losing their property and livelihoods at an epidemic rate.

JULY 22 — Flamboyant armed bank robber John Dillinger, the first criminal to be designated "Public Enemy No. 1" by J. Edgar Hoover's FBI, is gunned down by FBI agents outside the Biograph Theater in Chicago.

1935

MAY 6 — The most famous New Deal bureau, the Works Progress Administration (WPA), is created. Like the Public Works Administration which it replaces, the WPA is responsible for a wide array of public projects, ranging from massive road building and construction projects to federal support for the arts. At its peak in 1938, nearly 3,500,000 workers are on the WPA payroll.

MAY 27 — The controversial National Industrial Recovery Act is declared unconstitutional. The Supreme Court rules that the federal government has no authority to legislate prices, wages, and working conditions.

JUNE 10 — A New York stockbroker and an Ohio surgeon, both of whom had been habitual drunks, found Alcoholics Anonymous in Akron, Ohio as an organization to help other alcoholics recover. The organization spawns national chapters and becomes the best-known resource by which alcoholics seek to regain and maintain sobriety.

JULY 5 — FDR signs the National Labor Relations (Wagner-Connery) Act. The law establishes the National Labor Relations Board, with authority to recognize collective bargaining units, supervise union elections, and investigate allegations of illegal or unfair labor practices.

AUGUST 14 — FDR signs into law the Social Security Act, the most enduring piece of New Deal legislation. The Social Security Board, established by the act, manages payment of old-age benefits, which are determined by the amount of money a worker earns prior to age 65. A Social Security tax on wages provides funds from which the benefits are paid.

OCTOBER 10 — *Porgy and Bess* premieres at New York's Alvin Theater. With music by the innovative popular composer George Gershwin and a libretto by his brother Ira, and based on the novel by DuBose Heyward, the opera combines elements of folk traditions and popular music to tell the compelling story of a love triangle among the paraplegic Porgy, the beautiful Bess, and the brutal Crown, all of whom live in the black community of Charleston, South Carolina. Moderately successful in its first run, the opera becomes treasured as a groundbreaking classic of American music.

NOVEMBER 9 — Organizing dissident members of the American Federation of Labor, labor leader John L. Lewis founds the Committee for Industrial Organization (CIO). The new organization is intended to better represent unskilled industrial labor.

1936

EUGENE O'NEILL wins international recognition for the American stage when he accepts the Nobel Prize in literature for his dramas.

SEPTEMBER 30 — President Roosevelt dedicates Boulder Dam, construction of which had been authorized in 1928. The dam brings an end to the flood-and-drought cycle in a broad region of California, Arizona, New Mexico, and Nevada, allowing much more land to become productive and protecting residents of the area from natural disaster. Hydroelectric power generated by the 726-foot-high dam provides 4 billion kilowatt-hours of energy, enough electricity for 500,000 homes. Lake Mead, created by the dam, is a reservoir of 10 trillion gallons of water and covers 246 square miles. Built in the depths of the Great Depression, the dam is a prodigy of American engineering genius and the collective muscle, daring, and will of American workers. Boulder Dam will be renamed Hoover Dam (the name originally intended for it) in 1947.

NOVEMBER 3 — Roosevelt is reelected. His landslide over Republican Alf Landon attests to the overwhelming confidence of the American people in this extraordinarily charismatic and energetic leader.

1937

GERMAN-BORN AMERICAN PSYCHOANALYST Karen Horney, one of the great influx of German Jews who left the increasingly sinister environment of Germany in the late 1920s and early 1930s, publishes *The Neurotic Personality of Our Time,* a groundbreaking book that redefines Sigmund Freud's concept of neurosis not as aberrant disease but as the nearly inevitable product of contemporary civilization.

MAY 1 — With war clouds rapidly gathering over Europe, FDR signs the Neutrality Act of 1937, prohibiting the export of arms and ammunition to belligerent nations and barring U.S. ships from carrying war materiel for such nations.

MAY 6 — Americans are horrified by the sudden explosion of the German dirigible *Hindenburg* as it attempts to moor at Lakehurst, New Jersey. Some suspect sabotage of this, the pride of Nazi Germany's lighter-than-air fleet. Others point out that the ship was filled with highly explosive hydrogen, easily detonated by accident. The explosion ends the era of the great passenger-carrying dirigibles and spurs development of large passenger airplanes. It is also the first great manmade disaster to be covered live by radio broadcast.

DECEMBER 12 — The U.S. Navy gunboat *Panay* is sunk in Chinese waters by Japanese aircraft, killing two American sailors. Japan apologizes and makes reparations, but, dismissing U.S. protests, continues its war of invasion against China. This incident presages World War II in the Pacific.

1938

THORNTON WILDER'S innovative and influential *Our Town* is staged and is awarded a Pulitzer Prize. The play probes the lives of residents of a small New England village and is treasured as an evocative, poignant piece of Americana.

MAY 26 — The House Un-American Activities Committee (HUAC) is created by the U.S. House of Representatives to probe subversive activity in the U.S. government and public institutions, as well as in industry and business.

OCTOBER 30 — Orson Welles broadcasts his radio-play version of science-fiction novelist H. G. Wells's *The War of the Worlds.* The play is framed so realistically, and radio is by this time so pervasive and trusted a medium in the United States, that the play creates panic among many listeners who believe they are hearing actual news reports of an invasion by aliens from Mars.

1939

JANUARY 12 — With the world on the brink of war, President Roosevelt asks Congress for a record-shattering $535 million defense budget.

APRIL 30 — The 1939 World's Fair opens in New York. Brimming with the latest technology, the fair reflects a buoyant if misplaced optimism about the future of a world menaced by the growing tyranny of a ruthless cadre of European and Asian militarists and dictators.

AUGUST 24 — Politically savvy Americans are profoundly shocked by the news that, yesterday, Adolf Hitler and Joseph Stalin, the world's two most powerful dictators, had concluded a nonaggression pact.

SEPTEMBER 1 — At 4 a.m. (local time), German army and air forces invade Poland, effectively beginning World War II.

SEPTEMBER 3 — Twenty-eight Americans die when the British liner *Athenia* is sunk by a German submarine. Although the United States remains neutral, these are the first American casualties of World War II.

OCTOBER 2 — The United States and 20 other Pan-American nations proclaim their neutrality in the Declaration of Panama, while also announcing a 300-mile offshore "security zone" closed to the warships of belligerents. The declaration affirms the solidarity of the nations of the Western Hemisphere and puts the United States in the position of military protector of its neighbors.

OCTOBER 25 — Nylon stockings are first offered for sale in the United States as a replacement for stockings made from scarce silk.

NOVEMBER 4 — At FDR's urging, Congress passes a new Neutrality Act, repealing the provision of the Neutrality Act of 1937 that had barred arms exports to belligerent powers. The United States is now free to furnish arms to the anti-Axis powers, including Britain, France, and (after it joins the Allies in the summer of 1941) the Soviet Union, on a "cash and carry" basis.

DECEMBER 13–15 — *Gone with the Wind,* an epic film adapted from Margaret Mitchell's bestselling novel about the American Civil War, has a sensational three-day premiere in the story's focal point, Atlanta, Georgia.

1940

JUNE 22 — Americans are stunned by the rapid collapse of France under a German invasion. While the prospect of U.S. involvement in the "European war" remains overwhelmingly unpopular (more than 80 percent of Americans continue to favor neutrality), the public and politicians alike become increasingly aware that such involvement may be inevitable.

JUNE 28 — Congress passes the Alien Registration Act (the Smith Act), requiring the registration and fingerprinting of all aliens and outlawing membership in any organization advocating the overthrow of the United States.

SEPTEMBER 3 — The United States gives 50 obsolescent destroyers to Great Britain (which desperately needs convoy escort vessels) in exchange for 99-year leases on British naval and air bases in Newfoundland and the Caribbean.

SEPTEMBER 16 — Congress passes the Selective Service Act, the first peacetime military draft in American history.

NOVEMBER 5 — Franklin D. Roosevelt becomes the first president in U.S. history to be elected to a third term, defeating Republican Wendell L. Wilkie, 27,244,160 votes to 22,305,198.

DECEMBER 29 — In a speech, FDR proclaims that the United States will serve as the "arsenal of democracy" in aid of the Allies against the Axis. Some Americans decry this as warmongering, but most warily approve, and everyone is happy about the high level of lucrative employment the war production creates.

1941

MARCH 11 — Congress passes the Lend-Lease Act, giving the president authority to send, without requiring cash payment, arms and military equipment to any nation whose security he deems vital to the interests of the United States.

MARCH 17 — The National Gallery of Art opens in Washington, D.C., funded by a gift from financier Andrew W. Mellon.

JUNE 25 — With war looming, African-American civil rights leader A. Philip Randolph meets with FDR and warns him that unless he orders an end to racial discrimination in federal agencies and defense-related industries, Washington will find itself paralyzed by a mass protest march. FDR immediately responds with Executive Order 8802, prohibiting discrimination in all federal bureaus and defense plants. It is an early triumph in the American civil rights movement.

JULY 19 — At the urging of such social liberals as Eleanor Roosevelt, the U.S. Army Air Forces inaugurates a controversial program to train African-American men as military pilots. As in the rest of the U.S. military (which will not be racially integrated until 1948), the men are trained and serve in strictly segregated units. Later dubbed the "Tuskegee Airmen" (after the flight-training base set up at the all-black Tuskegee Institute in Alabama), the pilots go on to compile a brilliant combat record in the North African and Mediterranean theaters of World War II.

AUGUST 14 — Having secretly met and conferred aboard American and British warships anchored in Placentia Bay off the coast of Newfoundland, President Roosevelt and British prime minister Winston Churchill publish the product of their talks: the Atlantic Charter, a joint declaration of democratic principles that is just short of a formal Anglo-American military alliance against the Axis.

SEPTEMBER 11 — President Roosevelt orders American ships to attack German and Italian vessels found in "U.S. defensive waters." This marks the commencement of an undeclared naval war against the Axis.

OCTOBER 24 — The 40-hour workweek provision of the Fair Labor Act of 1938 goes into effect.

DECEMBER 7 — At 7:55 a.m. (local time) on a Sunday morning, a surprise attack on U.S. military installations at Pearl Harbor, Hawaii, decimates the U.S. Pacific Fleet, sinking five battleships and severely damaging three others along with three cruisers, three destroyers, and many smaller vessels. Some 180 aircraft are destroyed, and 2,403 sailors, soldiers, marines, and airmen are killed. It is a great tactical victory for Japan, but by thrusting the United States into World War II, it is also one of history's worst strategic blunders, ensuring the ultimate defeat not only of Japan but also of its Axis partners Germany and Italy.

DECEMBER 8 — U.S.-held Wake Island, Guam, and the Philippines all come under devastating Japanese attack shortly after the attack on Pearl Harbor. All will fall during the terrible early days, weeks, and months of what is now America's war.

DECEMBER 8 — In one of the 20th century's most famous speeches, President Roosevelt, calling the Japanese attack on Pearl Harbor on December 7 "a date which will live in infamy," asks a joint session of Congress for a declaration of war, which is overwhelmingly approved. The United States fights in World War II from this point until August 15, 1945.

DECEMBER 11 — Adolf Hitler's Germany and Benito Mussolini's Italy declare war on the United States, which responds with a reciprocal declaration against them.

1942

FEBRUARY 19 — President Roosevelt signs Executive Order 9066, authorizing the secretary of war to define military areas "from which any or all persons may be excluded as deemed necessary or desirable." Pursuant to the order, more than 100,000 Japanese Americans—U.S. citizens ("Nisei") as well as noncitizens ("Issei")—living on the American mainland within 200 miles of the Pacific Coast are "evacuated" to internment camps in California, Idaho, Utah, Arizona, Wyoming, Colorado, and Arkansas, where they spend most of the war. Many lose their homes and businesses.

FEBRUARY 25 — The military governor of Hawaii authorizes the formation of the Varsity Victory Volunteers, a group of 169 former University of Hawaii Reserve Officers' Training Corps (ROTC) students, all Japanese Americans eager to demonstrate their loyalty to the United States. The men dig ditches, build roads, and maintain military buildings. This leads to the creation of the 100th Infantry Battalion, the first all-Japanese-American combat unit in U.S. history. In 1943, the War Department creates the more famous all-Japanese-American 442nd Regimental Combat Team, which includes young men drawn directly from the internment camps. Fighting in Europe, the 442nd emerges as the army's most highly decorated unit for its size and time in service.

U.S. POPULATION: 131,669,275

APRIL 9 — The American surrender of Bataan signals the final fall of the Philippines and is followed by the infamous 100-mile Bataan Death March to a Japanese POW camp. Of the more than 60,000 U.S. and Filipino soldiers taken captive, between 7,000 and 10,000 die during the week-long march.

APRIL 18 — U.S. Army Air Forces colonel Jimmy Doolittle leads 16 twin-engine B-25 "Mitchell" bombers from the deck of the aircraft carrier *Hornet* on a spectacular air raid against Tokyo and other targets in Japan. The attack does little physical damage, but the boost to beleaguered American morale is thrilling and the injury to Japanese self-confidence stunning.

MAY — The first 29 Navajo Indian U.S. Marine Corps recruits report for basic training. They are destined to be trained as "code talkers"—marines who will employ in the front lines their complex Navajo language as the basis of a unique and unbreakable combat voice communications code.

MAY 7–8 — The Battle of the Coral Sea in the Pacific ends in a tactical (short-term) defeat for the U.S. Navy, but a strategic (long-term) defeat for the Japanese, whose Pacific juggernaut is permanently halted.

MAY 14 — Congress creates the Women's Army Auxiliary Corps (later shortened to Women's Army Corp, or WAC) under the command of Oveta Culp Hobby.

JUNE 4–6 — The Battle of Midway marks the turning point of the war in the Pacific. It is costly to U.S. Navy forces, but devastating to Japan, which loses four aircraft carriers, many planes, and many of its best pilots. From this point on, the United States seizes the offensive in the Pacific.

JULY 30 — Congress creates the WAVES (Women Accepted for Volunteer Emergency Service) in the U.S. Naval Reserve. The WAVES perform clerical and other non-combat duties both at home and overseas, thereby freeing more men for battle.

AUGUST 7 — Marines and soldiers land on Guadalcanal in the Solomon Islands. It is the first American ground offensive of the Pacific war and marks the beginning of a series of hard-fought island victories against an enemy of seemingly limitless determination.

NOVEMBER 8 — American forces make their first move in the Mediterranean theater with Operation Torch, the joint Anglo-American invasion of North Africa under the overall command of U.S. general Dwight D. Eisenhower.

1943

JANUARY 24 — The Casablanca Conference, between FDR and Churchill, concludes with an Allied agreement that nothing short of the unconditional surrender of the Axis powers will end the war.

JANUARY 27 — The U.S. Army Air Forces bomb Germany for the first time in the war. This marks the beginning of strategic bombing raids that will level many German cities but that will cost American aircrews more than 81,000 casualties, including 30,099 killed in action.

MARCH 2–4 — The U.S. Navy triumphs in the Battle of the Bismarck Sea, sinking a convoy of 22 Japanese ships and downing more than 50 enemy aircraft.

MAY 12 — The North African campaign ends in Allied victory as German and Italian forces withdraw from Africa.

JUNE 20 — Race riots erupt in Detroit when angry whites react to the wartime influx of African-American factory workers.

AUGUST 1 — U.S. bombers raid the oil fields and refineries at Ploesti, Romania. History's first large-scale, low-level strike by heavy bombers against a well-defended target, the raid distance is also the longest—1,350 miles from base to target—up to that time. Five fliers are awarded the Medal of Honor for the raid, a record that still stands. Of 179 B-24s launched, 55 are lost.

SEPTEMBER 8 — With Allied troops now fighting on its soil, Italy is the first of the Axis powers to surrender to the Allies.

DECEMBER 17 — President Roosevelt signs a bill repealing the Chinese Exclusion Acts. China is an important wartime ally of the United States.

DECEMBER 24 — Gen. Dwight D. Eisenhower is named supreme allied commander, Europe.

1944

JUNE 4 — Allied forces enter Rome. Although the Italians have surrendered, the city is still fiercely defended by German troops. It becomes the first Axis capital to fall.

JUNE 6 — More than 156,000 U.S., Canadian, and British troops land on the beaches of Normandy, France, as the "D-Day" invasion begins, with the objective of liberating France, then all western Europe, from Nazi occupation. It is the largest amphibious assault in the entire history of warfare.

JUNE 16 — The U.S. Army Air Forces begin an intensive campaign of strategic bombing against Japan.

JUNE 22 — Even as World War II continues to rage, Congress has begun to prepare for the return of American servicemen by passing the G.I. Bill (Servicemen's Readjustment Act), which FDR signs. The legislation provides extensive benefits for veterans, including generous mortgage assistance and educational scholarships.

AUGUST 21 — The Dumbarton Oaks Conference opens at a Georgetown (Washington, D.C.) mansion. Here representatives of the United States, Great Britain, China, and the Soviet Union lay the foundation for the United Nations.

AUGUST 25 — Paris is liberated from Nazi occupation by Allied troops, including Free French forces under Gen. Jacques-Philippe Leclerc.

OCTOBER 20 — U.S. forces led by Gen. Douglas MacArthur land at Leyte, Philippines redeeming the pledge MacArthur had made when he was evacuated from the islands at the beginning of the war: "I shall return." The invasion begins the arduous Philippines Campaign.

NOVEMBER 7 — FDR, reelected in 1940 to an unprecedented third term, is reelected to a fourth term. Exhausted and in visibly poor health, he nevertheless defeats Republican Thomas E. Dewey, 25,602,504 votes to 22,006,285.

DECEMBER 16 — Although German forces are in full retreat, Gen. Gerd von Rundstedt mounts a major offensive against thinly held U.S. positions in the Ardennes area of Luxembourg. This begins the Battle of the Bulge, the most desperate engagement of the European campaign. Caught by surprise and hampered by brutal winter weather, the Allies mount a counterattack. The U.S. Third Army under the brilliant and controversial George S. Patton, Jr., rescues the surrounded 101st Airborne Division, which has been holding the crucial town of Bastogne against vastly superior German numbers, and defeats the Germans—not only winning the Battle of the Bulge but breaking the back of the enemy army by mid-January 1945.

1945

FEBRUARY 4–11 — The Yalta Conference is held in the Crimea at which FDR, British prime minister Winston Churchill, and Soviet premier Joseph Stalin try to hammer out the postwar reorganization of a shattered Europe. The Yalta Conference yields a call for a conference to organize a United Nations, but also creates conditions that will bitterly and dangerously divide control of Europe between the Communist U.S.S.R. and the Western democracies.

MARCH 16 — Iwo Jima, a tiny volcanic island in the Pacific, falls to the United States after a bloody campaign by U.S. Marines. The island provides a key base for forward air operations against Japan.

APRIL 12 — In a terrible blow to the nation and its allies, President Franklin D. Roosevelt dies of a cerebral hemorrhage. Vice President Harry S. Truman assumes office.

MAY 7–8 — German field marshal Alfred Jodl signs the instrument of the unconditional surrender of German military forces at 2:41 a.m., May 7, at Reims, France, in the presence of U.S. general Walter Bedell Smith (representing Supreme Allied Commander Dwight D. Eisenhower) and a Soviet commander. The surrender is ratified at Berlin on May 8, the date which is now commemorated as Victory in Europe Day or V-E Day.

JUNE 21 — After a costly two-and-a-half-month campaign, Okinawa falls to marine and army forces. More than

100,000 Japanese defenders die on Okinawa. American losses include 13,000 killed and some 40,000 wounded. The fall of Okinawa opens the door to the Japanese home islands.

JULY 5 — The Philippines Campaign ends as the islands are declared secure.

JULY 16 — The first atomic bomb is successfully tested at Alamogordo, New Mexico. From even before U.S. entry into World War II, American and Allied scientists have been engaged in the enormous yet super-secret Manhattan Project to create highly destructive weapons based on nuclear fission.

JULY 28 — The United Nations, dedicated to providing a peaceful alternative to the resolution of international disputes, is chartered.

AUGUST 6 — *Enola Gay,* a U.S. Army Air Forces B-29 bomber, drops a single atomic bomb on Hiroshima, Japan. On August 9, another B-29, *Bock's Car,* drops an atomic bomb of different design on Nagasaki. The atomic age begins.

AUGUST 15 — Citing "a cruel new bomb," Japan's emperor Hirohito surrenders to the Allies, and World War II ends on "V-J Day." The formal instrument of surrender is signed aboard the U.S. battleship *Missouri* in Tokyo Bay on September 2.

1946

FEBRUARY 15 — Weighing in at more than 30 tons, ENIAC, the world's first fully electronic (vacuum-tube-based) computer begins operation at the University of Pennsylvania. The computer age commences.

MARCH 5 — Former British prime minister Winston Churchill, America's staunch ally in World War II, addresses an audience at Westminster College in Fulton, Missouri, and declares: "From Stettin in the Baltic to Trieste in the Adriatic, an iron curtain has descended across the continent." "Iron curtain" becomes the leading metaphor of Soviet Communist aggression in what develops as a 50-year Cold War.

JULY 7 — Mother Frances Xavier Cabrini is canonized by the Catholic Church as the first American saint.

1947

BRANCH RICKEY, president and general manager of the Brooklyn Dodgers baseball team, extends a contract to Jackie Robinson, who becomes the first African American to play on a modern major league team. At the start of the century, a few African Americans played briefly on white teams but were soon forced out, and black professional ballplayers were restricted to the segregated Negro Leagues. Robinson breaks "the color barrier" in professional baseball, and the integration of the sport is a prelude to racial integration on a national scale.

THE CONSTRUCTION FIRM of Levitt and Sons starts developing Levittown in Hempstead, Long Island, New York. By 1951, 17,450 homes are built there, housing 75,000 people. Levittowns (and similar projects by other builders) are developed elsewhere in the nation during the 1950s and 1960s. Houses are constructed of mass-produced prefabricated materials, which keeps construction costs low and makes the homes affordable. Construction time is also held to a minimum, enabling rapid production of homes for the burgeoning families of the post–World War II baby boom. The Levittown phenomenon transforms the American landscape and American postwar culture by turning the United States into an increasingly suburban nation.

APRIL 14 — In a speech, financier and presidential adviser Bernard Baruch coins the term "Cold War."

MAY 22 — President Harry S. Truman signs the Greek-Turkish Aid Bill, authorizing $400 million in aid to Greece and Turkey, which the United States vows to support against domination by Soviet-backed Communist forces. On signing the bill, Truman promulgates what becomes known as the Truman Doctrine, pledging the United States to "support free peoples who are resisting attempted subjugation by armed minorities or by outside pressure."

JUNE 5 — In a speech delivered at Harvard University, Secretary of State George C. Marshall proposes a sweeping economic plan to aid European recovery from World War II and thereby to block the expansion of Soviet influence on the European continent. The resulting "Marshall Plan" invests billions in aid to Europe and succeeds in promoting the political stability of the continent.

JUNE 23 — Over President Truman's veto, a probusiness Republican Congress passes the Taft-Hartley Act. Antilabor legislation that retracts the many labor union advantages created by the National Labor Relations Act of 1935, Taft-Hartley is a heavy blow to organized labor.

JULY 25 — Congress passes the National Security Act, which unifies the armed forces under a cabinet-level Department of Defense (replacing the War Department), authorizes the U.S. Air Force as a service arm independent of the U.S. Army, and creates the National Security Council and the Central Intelligence Agency (CIA).

OCTOBER 14 — Flying the Bell X-1, U.S. Air Force captain Charles Yeager becomes the first human being to fly faster than the speed of sound.

DECEMBER 3 — Tennessee Williams's *A Streetcar Named Desire* opens at the Ethel Barrymore Theater in New York City. It presents the story of Blanche Dubois, who finds herself adrift in the cold brutality of postwar American life. In addition to Blanche, the daring play gives the American stage Stanley Kowalski, a crude but vital embodiment of the life force. On stage, and later on film,

Kowalski is played by newcomer Marlon Brando, who is soon recognized as the most important young American actor of the postwar generation.

1947–1991

THE "COLD WAR" is the name given to the half-century contest between democracy and Communism, mainly as embodied by the United States and the Soviet Union, for domination of world politics. In the atomic age, the major powers recognize that all-out war will mean the destruction of civilization itself, so they wage instead a series of limited conflicts, some through propaganda, some through economic control, and some through "proxy wars"—wars of limited scale fought for control of smaller countries. President Truman sets the policy for the Cold War with the Truman Doctrine, which employs a strategy articulated by the State Department's George F. Kennan. The strategy is called "containment," the use of military means to meet communist aggression wherever and whenever it breaks, thereby containing communism while avoiding all-out nuclear war. Truman and others believe the strategy will buy sufficient time for the inherent superiority of democracy and capitalism to triumph over the innate weaknesses of communism and a command economy.

1948

JUNE 7 — The United States, France, and England announce their intention to create a new democracy, West Germany, from the parts of Germany they control. After

World War II, occupied Germany has been divided into four sectors controlled by those three nations and the Soviet Union. Now, the three western Allies plan to unite their sectors as a free nation in opposition to the Communist-controlled eastern lands. On June 24, Soviet forces respond by blockading West Berlin, which is to be part of the proposed new nation, even though it is nothing more than a democratically controlled enclave deep within the Soviet sector of Germany. Declaring that to give up West Berlin would mean relinquishing all of Germany to the Soviets, President Truman calls on the U.S. Air Force to organize a massive airlift to keep West Berlin supplied. Between June 26, 1948, and September 30, 1949, the air force makes 189,963 flights over Soviet-held territory into West Berlin (British forces make another 87,606 flights), resulting in a political triumph for the West when, on May 12, 1949, the Soviets lift the blockade. East and West Germany are created weeks later. The Berlin Airlift becomes the basis for the anti-Soviet North Atlantic Treaty Organization (NATO).

JUNE 25 — President Truman signs the Displaced Persons Act, opening immigration to 205,000 European war refugees. It is the first relaxation of immigration quotas in decades.

AUGUST 1948 — Whittaker Chambers, a self-confessed courier for a Communist espionage group, appears before the House Un-American Activities Committee (HUAC) and claims that Alger Hiss, a former State Department official in the FDR administration, has been a Soviet spy. Hiss denies the charges and is never indicted for espionage, but is indicted for perjury. A 1949 perjury trial ends in a hung jury, but he is convicted by a second jury and sentenced to five years' imprisonment. Released in 1954, Hiss, an early victim of the "Red baiting" and anti-communist hysteria that sweep the nation during the early years of the Cold War, spends the rest of his life trying to clear his name.

NOVEMBER 2 — Despite nearly universal predictions of victory for Republican Thomas E. Dewey, Harry S. Truman is reelected president, 24,104,836 votes to 21,969,500.

1949

WILLIAM FAULKNER, whose novels combine avant-garde literary techniques with a reverence for the timeless traditions of great storytelling and an abiding love of humanity, is awarded the Nobel Prize for literature.

FEBRUARY 10 — Arthur Miller's *Death of a Salesman* opens at New York's Morosco Theatre and garners, among many other honors, a Pulitzer Prize. It is the story of a worn-out salesman, Willie Loman, whose aspirations and failure say much about the American dream and capture the national disillusionment following the end of World War II.

APRIL 4 — Representatives of Belgium, Canada, Denmark, France, Great Britain, Iceland, Italy, Luxembourg, Netherlands, Norway, Portugal, and the United States sign the North Atlantic Treaty, creating the North Atlantic Treaty Organization, a mutual defense pact aimed against aggressive Soviet expansionism.

1950

JACKSON POLLOCK, a master of abstract expressionism, develops "action painting," a high-energy organic style that includes the technique of dripping pigment on the canvas, and establishes the internationally influential "New York School." America, not Europe, becomes the center of modern art.

TENNESSEE SENATOR Estes Kefauver opens congressional hearings on organized crime in America. The hearings expose the extent and pervasiveness of racketeering and other forms of organized crime. Televised, the hearings alter how Americans perceive their society, and they jolt the FBI into attacking a form of crime whose existence the bureau's director, J. Edgar Hoover, has long refused to recognize.

FEBRUARY 9 — Senator Joseph McCarthy, a Republican from Wisconsin, speaks at the Women's Republican Club of Wheeling, West Virginia, and waves a piece of paper before his audience, claiming that it lists the names of 205 Communists working for the U.S. Department of State. Although McCarthy later restates the number of Communists as 57, no one gets a look at the purported list, and the speech launches his reign as the leader of a national "witch hunt" aimed at rooting out purported

Communist agents in the nation's government, educational institutions, business enterprises, media corporations, and, eventually, the U.S. Army. Through endless hearings and accusations, McCarthy and his minions, most notoriously attorney Roy Cohn, identify no actual agents, but—through innuendo alone—manage to wreck many careers and even drive some individuals to suicide. The national paranoia over "Communist infiltration" reaches hysterical proportions.

JUNE 25 — Communist North Korean troops cross the 38th Parallel into Western-allied South Korea early in the morning, beginning the Korean War. The United States leads United Nations forces in a "police action" against the North Koreans, a brutal but limited war that ends inconclusively with an armistice on July 27, 1953.

SEPTEMBER 15 — Gen. Douglas MacArthur, hero of the Pacific theater of World War II, plans and executes the daring landing at Inchon, taking the North Korean forces by surprise and driving them to retreat far beyond the 38th Parallel. One of the great tactical and strategic achievements of 20th-century military history, the Inchon landing turns the tide of the Korean War—at least until Communist Chinese forces invade the country.

1950–1951

NOVEMBER 29, 1950–MARCH 1951 — As MacArthur carries the battle in the Korean War to the Yalu River—the border between North Korea and Chinese Manchuria—U.S.

president Harry S. Truman, anxious to avoid escalating the local conflict into World War III, cautions MacArthur to avoid provoking China's entry into the war. MacArthur assures Truman that China will not intervene, but, on November 29, 1950, overwhelming numbers of Communist Chinese troops cross the Yalu, driving the U.S.-dominated United Nations forces deep into South Korea, even capturing the South Korean capital, Seoul.

1951

FEBRUARY 26 — Congress adopts the 22nd Amendment, barring presidents from serving more than two terms. (On February 17, 2005, five Republican representatives introduced a bill to repeal the 22nd Amendment.)

MARCH 14 — U.S. forces in Korea retake Seoul.

APRIL 11 — In what is both the most courageous and most controversial decision of his presidency, Truman relieves Douglas MacArthur of command in Korea. MacArthur had demanded to expand the Korean War into China and even advocated using atomic weapons against the Chinese. When Truman insisted that MacArthur pursue a strategy of limited warfare consistent with the Truman Doctrine, MacArthur violated the chain of command by criticizing Truman and continuing to advocate all-out warfare, even wrecking scheduled peace talks by broadcasting an unauthorized ultimatum to the enemy prior to the talks. After

U.S. POPULATION: 150,697,361

being fired, MacArthur returns to a hero's welcome in the United States and delivers to Congress on April 19 a speech in which he asserts that "there is no substitute for victory" and then announces his retirement by quoting a traditional barracks ballad: "Old soldiers never die, they just fade away." In Korea, command of U.S. and UN forces is assumed by Matthew Ridgway, an excellent general with a keen appreciation of the limited war doctrine.

JUNE 14 — John W. Mauchly and J. Presper Eckert, Jr., who had developed ENIAC, the world's first all-electronic computer, unveil UNIVAC. It is the first major commercial electronic computer, and it launches the computer industry.

1952

NOVEMBER 1 — The United States detonates the first hydrogen bomb, dubbed "Mike," at 7:15 a.m. (local time) at Eniwetok Atoll in the Pacific. The "H-bomb" uses atomic *fission* (the "splitting" of an atomic nucleus) to create the energy that triggers nuclear *fusion*—the collision of neutrons with the nucleus of an unstable isotope of hydrogen under extremely high temperatures. The fusion reaction liberates even more energy than a fission reaction alone and therefore creates an explosion of far greater destructive force than that of an atomic (fission) bomb.

NOVEMBER 4 — Dwight D. Eisenhower, World War II's supreme allied commander in Europe, is elected president, defeating Democrat Adlai E. Stevenson by a very wide margin, 33,938,285 votes to 27,312,217. His vice president is Richard M. Nixon, who comes to office with a reputation as a hardcore anti-communist in the mold of Joe McCarthy.

1953

APRIL 1 — Congress creates the U.S. Department of Health, Education, and Welfare.

JUNE 19 — With the nation in the grip of an ongoing Cold War "Red scare," Julius and Ethel Rosenberg are executed for treason. In a case that has obsessed and divided the nation, the couple was convicted on March 29, 1951, of passing atom bomb secrets to Soviet agents. Their supporters variously believe them altogether innocent or at least insufficiently guilty to warrant the death penalty; many believe the Rosenbergs are victims of anti-Semitism. Their accusers, in contrast, believe them to be traitors who have endangered millions of innocent American lives. (Despite later claims by some former Soviet intelligence officials that the Rosenbergs did provide valuable information, the full extent of their guilt has never been definitively determined.)

JULY 27 — An armistice is signed at Panmunjom, North Korea, bringing an uneasy end to the Korean War and leaving the peninsula divided, along the 38th Parallel, between Communist North Korea and democratically aligned South Korea. A U.S. military presence remains on guard in the South.

1954

FEBRUARY 23 — Dr. Jonas Salk begins inoculating Pittsburgh, Pennsylvania, schoolchildren with the antipolio vaccine he has developed. The vaccine ends the cruel reign of a disease that has killed or crippled many thousands of children as well as many adults, including the late Franklin D. Roosevelt.

APRIL 23 – JUNE 17 — The U.S. Senate conducts the Army-McCarthy Hearings, investigating charges made by Senator Joseph McCarthy that Secretary of the Army Robert T. Stevens and others are attempting to hamper investigation of Communist infiltration of the U.S. military. The nationally televised hearings turn the tables on McCarthy, who is publicly exposed both as a reckless bully and as corrupt (he has tried to secure preferential treatment for a staff member, Pvt. G. David Schine). Public support for McCarthy dissolves, and his influence and power come to an end.

MAY 17 — In *Brown* v. *Board of Education of Topeka, Kansas*, the Supreme Court decides that racially segregated schools, even if the facilities provided are "separate but equal," are unconstitutional. The decision signals the beginning of the end to segregation in all aspects of American life. NAACP lawyer Thurgood Marshall, who argues the case, goes on to become the first African-American associate justice of the Supreme Court in 1967.

SEPTEMBER 30 — USS *Nautilus,* the world's first nuclear-powered submarine, is launched.

OCTOBER 28 — Novelist Ernest Hemingway is awarded the Nobel Prize for literature. His works probe the nature of courage and other powerful human motives. His style—muscular, minimalist, and immediate—redefines the art of narrative expression.

1954–1975

THE UNITED STATES' involvement in the Vietnam War—as in Korea, a struggle between the Communist north and the Western-aligned south—begins with military aid to bolster the badly faltering French colonial regime and, after the defeat of French forces, continues with military aid given directly to the government of South Vietnam. During the Eisenhower and Kennedy administrations, U.S. "military advisers" are sent to help South Vietnamese forces fight those of the North. Under President Lyndon B. Johnson, U.S. involvement reaches nearly a half-million combat troops in-country. The presidencies of both Johnson and Richard M. Nixon after him are plagued by the war and a desperate search for what Nixon calls "peace with honor." By 1975, 58,193 Americans have died in the Vietnam War, together with 223,748 South Vietnamese soldiers, 1.1 million North Vietnamese troops, and 2 million Vietnamese civilians.

1955

JANUARY 8 — Thorazine and Reserpine, so-called major tranquilizers, are introduced and revolutionize the treatment of mental illness by controlling behavior sufficiently to allow many patients to be treated outside of secure mental institutions. The introduction of these drugs ushers in an era of psychopharmacology.

DECEMBER 1 — Rosa Parks, an African-American seamstress and early civil rights activist, purposely violates a Montgomery, Alabama, city ordinance when she refuses to relinquish her bus seat to a white man. Her arrest triggers the Montgomery Bus Boycott, which lasts more than a year and forces the integration of the city's buses. The boycott is also the framework within which the early national civil rights movement is organized under the leadership of a young minister, Dr. Martin Luther King, Jr.

1956

JUNE 26 — At the urging of President Eisenhower, Congress passes the Interstate Highways Act, which funds construction of a national network of superhighways. The biggest public works project in the history of the United States, the Interstate Highway System by 2005 consists of about 160,000 miles of roadway serving every state of the Union.

SEPTEMBER 9 — Elvis Presley makes his first appearance on the *Ed Sullivan Show,* the most influential variety TV program of the 1950s. Singing "Don't Be Cruel," "Hound Dog," "Reddy Teddy," and "Love Me Tender," he is paid $50,000 for the appearance, a spectacular sum for the time, and intensifies the national sensation he has already created.

November 6 — Dwight D. Eisenhower is reelected president. The margin of the popular vote—35,387,015 to 25,875,408 for Democrat Adlai Stevenson—testifies to Ike's personal popularity, especially considering that the Democrats, not the Republicans, carry a majority of House and Senate seats in the election.

1957

SEPTEMBER 24 — President Eisenhower sends troops to enforce the federally mandated desegregation of public schools in Little Rock, Arkansas. Violent protest had barred nine black students from enrolling. They are escorted into the school and guarded there by U.S. Army paratroopers on September 25.

OCTOBER 4 — The successful launch of the first artificial Earth satellite, *Sputnik I,* by the Soviet Union stuns the United States, shaking many Americans out of a self-satisfied complacency that has often characterized the Eisenhower years. A "space race" begins, rapidly evolving into a contest to demonstrate the superiority of democratic capitalism over Soviet Communism.

1958

JANUARY 31 — After a series of embarrassing failures, the United States finally succeeds in orbiting a satellite of its own, *Explorer I.*

APRIL 11 — Twenty-three-year-old piano prodigy Van Cliburn, from Kilgore, Texas, wins the competition at the

Tchaikovsky International Piano and Violin Festival in Moscow, U.S.S.R. His triumph is a hopeful thaw in the bitter Cold War between the West and East and leads to a series of productive cultural exchanges.

1959

JANUARY 3 — After 92 years as a territory, Alaska becomes the 49th U.S. state.

JULY 23 — On a visit to the Soviet Union, Vice President Richard M. Nixon engages Soviet premier Nikita Khrushchev in the highly publicized "Kitchen Debate." While standing before a U.S.-sponsored exhibit of a modern American kitchen, intended to showcase the vast superiority of U.S. consumer goods over those available in the U.S.S.R., the two leaders good-naturedly debate the relative merits of life under democratic capitalism versus life under Soviet Communism.

AUGUST 21 — Hawaii becomes the 50th state. Annexed to the United States in 1898, Hawaii had been a U.S. territory since 1900.

1960

JANUARY 25 — Radio is rocked as the "payola scandal" comes to light. Donald H. McGannon, chairman of the review board of the National Association of Broadcasters, proposes a stiff federal law to fine and imprison disc jockeys guilty of accepting "payola"—recording company bribes to broadcast (and thereby promote) songs and records by particular artists. The scandal provokes a national debate on government regulation of the airwaves and the role of ethics in broadcasting.

FEBRUARY 23 — In a speech, Senator Stuart Symington, a Democrat from Missouri, challenges the existence of the "missile gap," claiming that the Eisenhower administration is deliberately misleading the American people. Throughout the 1950s, to spur accelerated development of America's arsenal of guided missiles with nuclear warheads, political and military leaders had frequently cited a widening missile gap between the Soviet Union and the United States. Symington's charge brings about a debate on the increasingly costly, frenzied, and dangerous arms race between the United States and the Soviet Union.

MAY 5 — The Soviets shoot down an unarmed Lockheed U-2 spy plane over their territory and subject its pilot, Francis Gary Powers, to a show trial on charges of espionage. At first, President Eisenhower denies that the aircraft was on a surveillance mission, but on May 7, he admits the truth. On May 9, the United States announces the discontinuance of U-2 flights; however, in a blow to U.S.–Soviet relations, the incident prompts Soviet premier Nikita Khrushchev to cancel the planned Paris summit with President Eisenhower and to withdraw an invitation for the president to visit the U.S.S.R.

MAY 9 — The U.S. Food and Drug Administration approves Enovid, the first birth control pill. "The pill" is highly effective in preventing conception and is widely credited with ushering in the "sexual revolution" of the 1960s.

NOVEMBER 8 — John F. Kennedy is elected president, defeating Republican Richard M. Nixon by a razor-thin margin of 0.1 percent of the popular vote. JFK is the nation's first Catholic president and, at 43, the youngest man elected to the office. (Theodore Roosevelt was 42 when he took office, but, as vice president, he had succeeded the slain McKinley and was not elected in his own right until later.)

1961

JANUARY 28 — The Peace Corps is announced. Endorsed by President Kennedy, the organization soon sends young people to Third World nations to assist at the grassroots level in development and antipoverty projects. It is part of a campaign to impart the best of American values to the developing world, regions vulnerable to Communist influence.

APRIL 17 — Approximately 1,500 anti-Castro Cuban exiles, trained by the CIA and organized by an American-based anti-Castro group (the National Revolutionary Council) land in Cuba at the Bay of Pigs. Catastrophically poor CIA intelligence has suggested that the Cuban people will spontaneously rise up and join the exiles in overthrowing Fidel Castro; instead, the invasion meets with overwhelming resistance, the U.S. government fails to furnish additional support, and the

Bay of Pigs invasion ends in humiliating defeat, for which President Kennedy publicly accepts full responsibility. Eventually, the surviving invaders are released in exchange for a large U.S. shipment of medicines badly needed by Cuba.

MAY 5 — Alan Bartlett Shepard, Jr., becomes the first American in space, flying a 15-minute suborbital mission in his space capsule, *Freedom 7*. Soviet cosmonaut Yuri Gagarin had beaten Shepard into space with a full-scale orbital flight in *Vostok I* on April 12.

JUNE 3–4 — JFK and Soviet premier Nikita Khrushchev meet (with surprising cordiality) at the Vienna Summit to discuss nuclear disarmament, Berlin, and the fate of Laos.

1962

FEBRUARY 14 — Jacqueline Kennedy, the president's understatedly glamorous wife, conducts a unique televised tour of the White House. Her purpose is to show the American people "their" house and generate support for her program of restoration. The nation is favorably impressed by "Jackie," who comes to be regarded as the American equivalent of royalty.

FEBRUARY 20 — U.S. Marine major (later, colonel) John Glenn is the first American to orbit the Earth.

FEBRUARY 26 — The Supreme Court rules unconstitutional all laws creating or protecting segregation in interstate transport. This forces the integration of buses, trains, and all station facilities.

JULY 10 — Telstar, the first communications satellite, is launched. Although manned spaceflight grabs the biggest headlines, Telstar (a joint project of AT&T and Bell Laboratories) is one of the most important American space projects, the first experiment in satellite relay—today indispensable to the world's vast communications, broadcast, data, and navigational (GPS) networks.

SEPTEMBER 30 — Escorted by federal marshals, James H. Meredith becomes the first African American to enroll at the University of Mississippi. White protest is violent: a riot, in which two die, is quelled by 3,000 troops.

OCTOBER 22 — In an urgent televised broadcast, President Kennedy tells the nation that the Soviet Union is building nuclear missile and bomber bases in Cuba, 90 miles from Key West, Florida. JFK authorizes a naval blockade (calling it a "quarantine") of Cuba, effective October 24, to prevent further shipment of offensive weapons. The Organization of American States (OAS) unanimously endorses the use of armed force to prevent Cuban importation of offensive weapons. On October 25, Adlai Stevenson, U.S. ambassador to the United Nations, exhibits aerial reconnaissance photos showing missile installations. The same day, U.S. Navy crew

U.S. POPULATION: 179,245,000

members board and inspect a Soviet ship bound for Cuba. The "Cuban Missile Crisis" looms as a flashpoint for nuclear warfare between the two superpowers, the United States and U.S.S.R. Over the next several days, American schoolchildren practice daily air raid drills in anticipation of an all-out missile attack, and churches fill to overflowing with those praying for peace. Ultimately, however, an adroit combination of formal and backdoor diplomacy defuses the situation, as Soviet premier Khrushchev agrees on October 27 to remove the missiles from Cuba in exchange for an unofficial pledge that the United States will remove its nuclear missiles stationed in Turkey, and, on October 28, JFK and Khrushchev conclude a formal agreement for the withdrawal of the Cuban missiles and the institution of UN inspections in exchange for a promise by the United States that it will not invade Cuba. The Cuban Missile Crisis also motivates Khrushchev and Kennedy to open direct communications between Moscow and Washington, resulting in the "hot line," which goes into effect on August 30, 1963.

1963

FREELANCE JOURNALIST BETTY FRIEDAN publishes *The Feminine Mystique,* a book documenting aspects of the lives of her fellow Smith College graduates and exposing the profound intellectual and spiritual discontents many women suffer in their attempt to live according to the socially prescribed conventions of domesticity, child bearing, and child rearing. The bestseller is credited with sparking the feminist movement of the 1960s. In 1966, Friedan founds NOW, the National Organization for Women, a group that fosters equal rights and opportunities for women in the workplace and elsewhere.

JUNE 12 — Civil rights leader Medgar Evers is gunned down outside his Jackson, Mississippi, home. The assassination sparks nationwide outrage in black as well as white communities.

JUNE 26 — President Kennedy visits Berlin, the city divided between East and West in the heart of Soviet-controlled East Germany. In a speech before a crowd of more than 100,000 West Berliners, JFK proclaims, "Ich bin ein Berliner"—*I am a Berliner*—a pledge of America's enduring solidarity with the courageous city and the principles of liberty for which it stands.

AUGUST 29 — Some 200,000 people participate in the Freedom March on Washington and gather at the National Mall to hear speeches by the nation's civil rights leaders. The Reverend Dr. Martin Luther King, Jr., delivers the most celebrated speech of his career and of the entire civil rights movement, declaring, "I have a dream" and sharing his vision of an America free from racial injustice.

SEPTEMBER 15 — In one of the most horrific acts of violence during the civil rights era, four young girls are killed when the 16th Street Baptist Church, an African-American church serving (like many other black churches) as a center for civil rights activity, is bombed in Birmingham, Alabama. The bombing touches off riots in which two more persons are killed and 19 injured.

OCTOBER 7 — In a significant if tentative stride toward nuclear arms control, President Kennedy signs the Nuclear Test Ban Treaty. The Soviet Union, the United States, and other nations agree to end atmospheric test detonations of nuclear and thermonuclear devices, restricting all testing to underground explosions.

NOVEMBER 22 — While visiting Dallas, Texas, President John Fitzgerald Kennedy is assassinated. Texas governor John B. Connally, riding in the president's limousine, is grievously wounded as well. The president dies at 1 p.m. (local time), and Vice President Lyndon B. Johnson is sworn in as president at 2:39 p.m. aboard Air Force One, which is parked at Love Field, Dallas. Lee Harvey Oswald is arrested later in the day (after shooting and killing a Dallas police officer) and accused of having shot the president, sniper style, from a window of the Texas School Book Depository Building. While he is being transferred from Dallas police headquarters to jail on November 24, Oswald is shot by Jack Ruby, a mob-connected Dallas nightclub owner. Although reliable evidence points to Oswald as the lone gunman, his sudden death leaves many questions unanswered and leads to decades of speculation about larger conspiracies that might have been responsible for the president's murder.

1964

JANUARY 11 — U.S. Surgeon General Luther Terry issues a report concluding that cigarette smoking "contributes substantially to mortality from certain specific diseases and to the overall death rate." The "Surgeon General's Report" begins a long government assault on one of the nation's oldest and largest industries.

JANUARY 23 — South Dakota becomes the 38th state to ratify the 24th Amendment. The amendment, aimed at ensuring the enfranchisement of poor people, especially African Americans, abolishes all poll taxes.

FEBRUARY 25 — Cassius Clay (who soon takes the name Muhammad Ali) wins the world heavyweight boxing crown, defeating the formidable and much-feared Sonny Liston. Ali goes on to successfully defend his title 19 times and is regarded by many as the greatest boxer of all time. His association with the Nation of Islam ("Black Muslims") and his refusal to be inducted into the army during the Vietnam War later bring public criticism and criminal prosecution—as well as admiration in the black and antiwar communities. In 1967, Ali is stripped of his title and barred from boxing (a ban that lasts three and a half years). He returns to the ring in 1970 and the Supreme Court reverses his criminal conviction in 1971, but his most enduring impact on American society is conveyed in his example and message of black pride and resistance to white oppression.

JULY 2 — The Civil Rights Act, the proudest achievement of the LBJ administration, is signed. It extends civil rights into virtually all sectors of American life, banning racially based segregation and discrimination in all public accommodations, such as theaters and restaurants, and in hiring and other job practices.

AUGUST 2 — The U.S. Navy destroyer *Maddox,* conducting electronic surveillance in international waters, reports being attacked by North Vietnamese torpedo boats. Undamaged, the *Maddox* is joined by a second destroyer, the *C. Turner Joy,* and on August 4, both ships report coming under fire. In response, President Johnson orders retaliatory air strikes against North Vietnam, and, at his request, on August 7, the U.S. Senate passes the Gulf of Tonkin Resolution, giving the president virtually unlimited authority to escalate U.S. military involvement in Vietnam. (In 1971, the "Pentagon Papers" reveal the attacks on the destroyers were actually a provocation at least partially fabricated by the Johnson administration.)

AUGUST 4 — The bodies of James Chaney, Andrew Goodman, and Michael Schwerner, young men engaged in civil rights and voter registration work in Mississippi, are found buried outside of Philadelphia, Mississippi. Of the three victims, only Chaney is African American and a Mississippian. Goodman and Schwerner are white New Yorkers, volunteers for the Congress of Racial Equality (CORE). Federal authorities arrest 19 men, including a sheriff and his deputy, for the murders. On October 20, 1967, seven of those charged and tried are convicted and given sentences ranging from three to ten years. (In 2005, 80-year-old Edgar Ray Killen, a former KKK leader, is retried for his role in the murders and found guilty of three counts of manslaughter on June 21.)

SEPTEMBER 27 — The Warren Commission, convened by LBJ to investigate the Kennedy assassination and led by Supreme Court chief justice Earl Warren, publishes its report, concluding that Lee Harvey Oswald was the sole assassin and was not part of a larger conspiracy. Intended to lay to rest all questions relating to the assassination, the report serves only to fuel the debate over conspiracy.

NOVEMBER 3 — Lyndon B. Johnson is elected president in his own right, defeating Republican Barry Goldwater, widely perceived as a right-wing extremist who would not only escalate the Vietnam War but possibly use it to start World War III. Johnson wins by a stunning landslide: 43,126,506 votes to 27,176,799.

1964–1968

JOHN F. KENNEDY had an ambitious civil rights and social reform agenda, but was unable to muster congressional support for most of his program before he was assassinated. Lyndon Johnson, his successor, uses what he skillfully characterizes as the martyrdom of JFK to gain the support that had eluded Kennedy, pushing through

Congress a series of laws that transforms American life. He calls them, collectively, the Great Society. As the U.S. commitment to the Vietnam War increases, however, funding for the Great Society is reduced, and many of the programs falter and fail.

1965

RALPH NADER, a young attorney and pioneering consumer advocate, publishes *Unsafe at Any Speed,* citing Chevrolet's Corvair as an egregious example of the unsafe and unreliable automobiles offered to American consumers. The book motivates legislation to mandate safer automobiles and initiates a consumer-awareness and consumer-protection movement throughout the United States.

FEBRUARY 21 — Malcolm X, among the most eloquent, charismatic, and controversial leaders to emerge during the civil rights movement, is assassinated by rival members of the Black Muslims as he addresses an audience at the Audubon Ballroom in New York's Harlem. Aggressively militant in the early phase of his association with the Black Muslims, Malcolm X had originally advocated empowerment for blacks *and* segregation from whites, whom he called "devils"; deeper exploration of Islam, however, moved him away from his extreme anti-white stance, and he began to look for an alternative both to violence as well as what he perceived as the overly passive nature of Martin Luther King's nonviolence. *The Autobiography of Malcolm X,* published in 1965, is an enduring and influential document of the black American experience.

MARCH 7 — John Lewis, head of the Student Nonviolent Coordinating Committee (SNCC, a civil rights group), and fellow activist Hosea Williams lead marchers from the Brown Chapel AME Church to the foot of the Edmund Pettus Bridge in Selma, Alabama. Local police respond with extreme violence in a police riot known as "Bloody Sunday." Footage of the police action is broadcast nationally, and demonstrations in support of the marchers are held in 80 cities. On March 9, Martin Luther King, Jr., leads another group to the Pettus Bridge, where they kneel in prayer. That night a white Northern minister and supporter of the marchers, James Reeb, is fatally clubbed by white vigilantes. Beginning on March 21, King leads a nationally publicized five-day march from Selma to Montgomery, Alabama, the state capital.

MARCH 8–9 — President Johnson commits the first U.S. ground combat forces—3,500 marines—to the Vietnam War. (U.S. Air Force personnel—ostensibly not involved in ground action—and U.S. Army "advisers"—ostensibly not involved in active combat—have been serving in Vietnam since the Eisenhower administration.)

AUGUST 6 — In large measure spurred by the violence in Selma, Alabama, Congress passes and LBJ signs the Voting Rights Act of 1965. This Great Society act outlaws literacy tests and other means by which some states and local jurisdictions attempt to restrict voting, especially among African Americans and especially in the South.

AUGUST 11–16 — The arrest of a black motorist on suspicion of drunk driving sparks a riot in the Watts section of Los Angeles. Despite passage of important civil rights legislation, race relations have generally deteriorated during the 1960s, and the ghettos of American cities routinely erupt into race riots during what the media calls "the long, hot summer" of 1965. The Watts riot is among the worst. Thirty-five are killed and many hundreds injured. Property damage tops $200 million.

SEPTEMBER 6 — Cesar Chavez leads migrant farmworkers in a strike against California grape growers and calls for a national consumer boycott of California table grapes in an effort to force growers to recognize the United Farm Workers union. Chavez brings both Hispanic Americans and migrant laborers (most of whom are Hispanic) under the civil rights umbrella and helps to give these groups a voice in American policy and politics.

1966

JANUARY 17 — Congress confirms President Johnson's appointment of Robert C. Weaver as secretary of the newly created Department of Housing and Urban Development. Weaver is the first African American to hold a cabinet seat.

JUNE 13 — The United States Supreme Court rules in the case of *Miranda* v. *State of Arizona.* Lawyers from the American

Civil Liberties Union appeal the 1963 conviction of Ernesto Miranda for rape, on the basis of the failure of the police to inform Miranda of his Fifth Amendment right to avoid self-incrimination by refusing to answer police questions without the presence of legal counsel. The Supreme Court overturns the conviction, and, as a result of the Miranda decision, arresting officers are now required to read suspects their "Miranda rights," informing them that they have the right to remain silent and to have an attorney present before any questioning is conducted. (As for Miranda, he is subsequently retried and convicted on new evidence.)

JULY 14 AND AUGUST 1 — Two horrific instances of senseless violence are dubbed by some the "crimes of the century": On July 14, Richard Franklin Speck, a drifter, brutally murders eight student nurses in their Chicago apartment. (A ninth student nurse, who witnesses the murders, saves herself by rolling under a bed.) Then on August 1, Charles J. Whitman ascends the University of Texas clock tower in Austin and, using a sniper rifle, kills 13 persons and wounds another 13 before police kill him. Prior to ascending the tower, he had already killed his wife and his mother. Many horrified Americans interpret these crimes as symptoms of the amoral and bewildering nature of contemporary life.

1967

JANUARY 15 — The first annual Superbowl is played, between the National Football League's Green Bay Packers and the American Football League's Kansas City Chiefs. The Packers win, 35–10, and the Superbowl evolves into a sport-and-media event of huge and hugely profitable proportions.

FEBRUARY 10 — Nevada becomes the 38th state to ratify the 25th Amendment, which specifies the succession of presidential authority in cases of death, resignation, or incapacity.

MARCH 1 — The House of Representatives votes 307 to 116 to deny Representative Adam Clayton Powell of New York his House seat. Powell is under investigation for misusing $46,000 of government-appropriated money for private purposes; however, many African Americans and liberal whites see the censure as an attempt to silence a high-profile and often discordant black legislative voice.

JUNE 30 — GATT (the General Agreement on Tariffs and Trade) is signed in Geneva, Switzerland, by the United States and 45 other nations. GATT promotes international free trade and is an important step in the increasing globalization of the marketplace.

OCTOBER 2 — Thurgood Marshall becomes the first African American sworn in as a Supreme Court associate justice.

1968

JANUARY 23 — USS *Pueblo,* a lightly armed naval intelligence-gathering ship, is seized by North Korea off its coast. In an incident humiliating to the United States, its 83-member crew is held until December 23, when their release is negotiated. The *Pueblo* itself is never returned.

JANUARY 30–FEBRUARY 24 — Beginning on January 30, the first day of the Vietnamese lunar holiday called Tet, North Vietnamese forces stage a massive offensive consisting of attacks against South Vietnamese provincial capitals and other cities, as well as American and ARVN (Army of the Republic of Vietnam) bases and strong points. The attacks continue through February 24 and, while costly to U.S. and South Vietnamese forces, are far more costly to the attackers. Militarily, the defense against the Tet Offensive is a U.S.–South Vietnamese victory, but most Americans on the home front perceive it as a Communist triumph or, at the very least, a dramatic demonstration of the North's will to continue the war regardless of its losses. The Tet Offensive continues to turn American public opinion against the Vietnam War.

MARCH 16 — Lt. William Calley, Jr., leads a U.S. infantry unit in a massacre at My Lai 4, a village in Songmy, South Vietnam. His unit kills 450 villagers, including women, children, and infants. The My Lai Massacre is first reported by national news media on November 12, 1968. Calley is convicted on March 29, 1971, of the murder of 22 people. All others, above and below him, are exonerated, leading to charges that Calley, who is sentenced to life imprisonment, is being scapegoated. Calley's sentence is repeatedly reduced, and he is finally paroled in November 1974.

MARCH 31 — In a televised address, Lyndon Johnson announces a partial halt to the bombing of North Vietnam, the opening of peace negotiations, and his intention not to run for reelection.

APRIL 4 — The Reverend Dr. Martin Luther King, Jr., is assassinated by a sniper in Memphis, Tennessee. Urban riots in many cities follow the murder of the apostle of nonviolent change. The accused sniper is James Earl Ray, who confesses to the crime and pleads guilty but later recants. Despite compelling evidence that paints Ray as the lone gunman, some, including members of the King family, believe he has been sacrificed to cover up a broader conspiracy, perhaps involving agencies of the U.S. government. Ray dies in prison, of liver failure, on April 23, 1998.

APRIL 11 — The Civil Rights Act of 1968 is signed by President Johnson. It mandates equal opportunity in housing and prohibits racial discrimination in the sale or rental of dwellings.

JUNE 4–5 — The withdrawal of LBJ from the 1968 presidential race leaves the possibility of an avowedly antiwar candidate gaining the Democratic nomination. Winning in the June 4 California primaries, Senator Robert F. Kennedy, brother of the late John Fitzgerald Kennedy, emerges as an antiwar frontrunner. After thanking his supporters gathered in the ballroom of the Ambassador Hotel in Los Angeles at about 12:15 on the morning of June 5, Kennedy makes his way through a kitchen area behind the ballroom. There he is shot in the head at close range by Sirhan Sirhan, a Jordanian national. His wound is fatal.

AUGUST 26–29 — In a year marked by assassination, riot, and the ongoing mayhem of Vietnam, the Democratic Convention in Chicago becomes the scene of mass violence as Chicago police and members of the National Guard clash with large numbers of antiwar protestors. In full view of network television cameras, police lash out, indiscriminately beating protestors—some of whom are belligerent, others peaceful—along with bystanders and news reporters, transforming a protest disturbance into a full-scale police riot. The convention nominates Hubert H. Humphrey, who does not oppose the Vietnam War.

NOVEMBER 5 — Richard M. Nixon, vice president under Eisenhower, is elected president, defeating Democrat Hubert H. Humphrey in a close election: 31,785,480 popular votes to 31,275,166. Third-party segregationist candidate George C. Wallace garners 9,906,473 votes.

1969

THE U.S. DEPARTMENT OF DEFENSE launches ARPANET (Advanced Research Projects Agency Network) to connect Defense Department computers with those of other government agencies and with universities, defense contractors, and other institutions doing defense-related work. This network becomes the basis from which the Internet develops.

JUNE 27 — Shortly after 1 a.m., New York City police officers and agents of the city's Alcoholic Beverage Control Board enter the Stonewall Inn, ostensibly in search of violations of liquor ordinances, but actually to roust patrons. Like other gay bars in New York City's Greenwich Village, the Stonewall is frequently the target of police harassment during the 1960s. In the past, such treatment met with little or no resistance. This morning, however, it triggers a 3-day riot often cited as the founding event of the gay rights movement in the United States.

JULY 20 — *Apollo 11,* carrying astronauts Neil A. Armstrong, Edwin E. "Buzz" Aldrin, and Michael Collins, is launched on July 16. At 4:17 p.m. EDT. on July 20, the spacecraft's lunar excursion module (LEM), called *Eagle,* touches down on the moon. A short time later, Armstrong climbs down *Eagle*'s ladder and becomes the first human being to set foot on Earth's natural satellite. "That's one small step for [a] man," he says, "and one giant leap for mankind." Aldrin follows Armstrong, and the two gather geological specimens and make other observations for the next two hours. Throughout, live television pictures are transmitted to hundreds of millions of viewers on Earth.

AUGUST 9 — Actress Sharon Tate (wife of filmmaker Roman Polanski) and four others are found brutally murdered in the Polanski-Tate home. It is discovered that they are victims of Charles Manson and his small cult of followers, who also murder two other victims, Leno and Rosemary

LaBianca, in another house. To many Americans, Manson and his cult reveal the dark side of the hippie counterculture that has developed during the 1960s, a culture (as some see it) of communal living, general lawlessness, drug use, and ultimate anarchy.

AUGUST 15–18 — If the Manson murders represent the dark side of America's counterculture, the Woodstock Festival in New York's Catskills area, an outdoor rock and folk music concert, is seen by many as an example of all that is positive about the ethic of free love and the spirit of communality. Some 300,000–400,000 people gather for the festival, which, though plagued by rain and poor planning, is nevertheless suffused in a drug-enhanced atmosphere of peace and love that seems the ultimate expression and celebration of the positive values of 1960s youth culture.

SEPTEMBER 24 — The trial of the Chicago Eight begins. Rennie Davis, David Dellinger, John Froines, Tom Hayden, Abbie Hoffman, Jerry Rubin, Bobby Seale, and Lee Wiener, all prominent radical leaders, are accused of having conspired to incite riots during the 1968 Democratic National Convention. They claim they are being prosecuted for their political views. Seale's courtroom behavior sends him to prison for contempt, and the case is continued against the rest, who are now called the Chicago Seven. The trial ends on February 18, 1970, with acquittals on the conspiracy charges, but five defendants are found guilty of crossing a state line with intent to incite a riot and are sentenced to five-year prison terms. The convictions are overturned on appeal in 1972 because of Judge Julius Hoffman's many procedural errors and his overt hostility toward the defendants. In 1972, the contempt charges against Seale are also set aside.

OCTOBER 28 — Senator J. William Fulbright, who chairs the Senate Foreign Relations Committee, charges that the Nixon administration is conducting an illegal war in Laos (which borders Vietnam) without the knowledge or consent of Congress.

NOVEMBER 24 — President Nixon ratifies the Nuclear Non-Proliferation Treaty with the Soviet Union.

1970

APRIL 22 — The first Earth Day is observed across the United States, raising public awareness of environmental issues.

MAY 4 — President Nixon's announcement that he is expanding the Vietnam War into neighboring Cambodia ignites a new wave of antiwar demonstrations across the country. At Kent State University in Ohio, demonstrators set fire to the ROTC building, and the governor calls out 900 National Guardsmen. In a confrontation with rock-throwing students, some inexperienced troops fire into the demonstrators, killing four. The action is publicly and officially condemned, and support for the war, waning daily, plummets further.

MAY 9 — In the wake of the Kent State shootings, some 100,000 antiwar protestors march on Washington. This massive demonstration is accompanied by others throughout the country. Never before have so many Americans united so decisively in protesting a war.

SEPTEMBER 30 — *The New American Bible* is published. A modern milestone in religious publication and biblical scholarship, the new Bible is the first English-language Roman Catholic-sponsored translation of scripture based directly on the original sources.

DECEMBER 2 — President Nixon issues an executive order creating the Environmental Protection Agency (EPA) to draft and enforce environmental standards for a broad array of products, projects, and activities. The agency also identifies and oversees the cleanup of pollution hazards.

1971

MARCH 1 — Radical dissidents belonging to an antiwar, anti-Nixon, and anti-Establishment organization known as the Weather Underground bomb the U.S. Capitol. The bomb, planted in the Senate wing, causes about $300,000 of damage, but injures no one.

JUNE — The *New York Times* commences publication of a long series of articles collectively known as the "Pentagon Papers." The massive, top-secret document, officially titled The *History of the U.S. Decision Making Process in Vietnam,* had been commissioned by Robert S. McNamara, the secretary of defense during the Kennedy administration and part of the Johnson administration, and has been leaked to the *Times* by one of its disaffected authors, Daniel Ellsberg. It reveals a tragic web of error, confusion, misconception, misjudgment, and deliberate, unconstitutional acts of deception that have drawn the nation more and more deeply into Vietnam beginning as early as the administration of Harry S. Truman. The revelations are profoundly shocking, reaching to the very core of American government. The Nixon administration acts against Ellsberg and the *New York Times,* but all attempts to block further publication of the "Pentagon Papers" are overturned by the U.S. Supreme Court, which cites the First Amendment right of free speech.

JUNE 30 — Ohio becomes the 38th state to ratify the 26th Amendment, which lowers the legal voting age from 21 to 18.

1972

FEBRUARY 21–28 — In an epoch-making gesture, President Nixon visits China and meets with Chairman Mao Zedong. The two leaders jointly issue the Shanghai Communiqué on February 27, agreeing to work together to reduce the potential for war, to normalize economic and diplomatic relations, and to develop mutually beneficial scientific and cultural ties.

MARCH 22 — Congress approves the Equal Rights Amendment, the proposed 27th Amendment, and submits it to the states for ratification. The measure, which was written in 1921 by radical American feminist Alice Paul, would prohibit discrimination on account of sex.

MAY 2 — J. Edgar Hoover, for five decades head of the Federal Bureau of Investigation (FBI), dies in his sleep. Hoover had transformed the small, ineffective, and corrupt Bureau of Investigation into the FBI, the most famous and well-respected law enforcement agency in the world. At the same time, he amassed personal power, covertly compiling dossiers on government officials, public figures, and others. The secret knowledge he wielded made him a kind of shadow president, and the FBI, at times, functioned as a secret police force operating beyond the margins of the Constitution.

MAY 8 — As a part of a strategy of simultaneously reducing American ground forces in Vietnam while escalating the intensity of the war, President Nixon orders the mining of Haiphong Harbor and other North Vietnamese ports. On the home front, this serves to heighten antiwar sentiment.

JUNE 17 — Five "burglars" are arrested for a break-in at Democratic Party Headquarters in Washington's Watergate complex. Investigative reporting by two young *Washington Post* reporters, Bob Woodward and Carl Bernstein, reveals that they are agents of Nixon's White House, so-called Plumbers (responsible for plugging "leaks" in the wake of the "Pentagon Papers" scandal), who were attempting to bug Democratic Party communications. The arrests begin the unraveling of a massive, covert, and unconstitutional system of surveillance, political sabotage ("dirty tricks"), and intimidation, which reaches into every level of the executive branch, including the Department of Justice and the president himself. The Watergate scandal ultimately brings down the president.

SEPTEMBER 1 — Bobby Fischer wins the world chess championship, triumphing over Boris Spassky of the Soviet Union in play at Reykjavik, Iceland.

NOVEMBER 7 — Despite the early rumblings of the Watergate scandal, Richard Nixon is reelected, easily defeating Democrat George S. McGovern, 45,767,218 votes to 28,357,668. The Democrats, however, retain control of both houses of Congress.

DECEMBER 18 — As peace negotiations between North Vietnam and the United States stall in Paris, President Nixon orders the "Christmas Bombing" of North Vietnam.

1973

January 17 — The Paris Peace Accords are signed. The agreement among North and South Vietnam and the United States calls for a cease-fire, withdrawal of U.S. troops, release of all POWs, and the peaceful reunification of North and South Vietnam. In fact, the accords are routinely violated, and the war continues until the fall of Saigon, on April 30, 1975.

U.S. POPULATION: 203,982,000

JANUARY 22 — The U.S. Supreme Court hands down a decision in *Roe* v. *Wade,* holding that state laws barring abortion during the first six months of pregnancy violate a woman's "right to privacy," which, the court asserts, is constitutionally protected. The controversial decision galvanizes the ongoing battle between passionate advocates and opponents of "abortion rights."

JANUARY 27 — Secretary of Defense Melvin Laird announces an end to the military draft.

FEBRUARY 28 — Members of the American Indian Movement (AIM), occupy Wounded Knee, South Dakota, scene of the 1890 Wounded Knee Massacre. AIM occupies it to draw attention to its demands for an investigation of the Bureau of Indian Affairs, the right to freely elect tribal leaders, and a review of all U.S.–Indian treaties. The occupation ends on May 8 when government officials promise action on Indian grievances.

APRIL 2 — Officials of the International Telephone & Telegraph Corporation reveal that IT&T had offered to fund a CIA-engineered overthrow of Marxist Chilean president Salvador Allende Gossens, who was elected in 1970. It is a stunning revelation of the intervention of American big business in national and international political affairs. On September 11, 1973, Allende is assassinated in a military coup d'état.

OCTOBER 10 — Vice President Spiro T. Agnew becomes the first major figure to fall in the scandal-plagued Nixon administration. After pleading no contest to a charge of income tax evasion brought against him, he resigns in disgrace.

OCTOBER 17 — OPEC, the Organization of Petroleum Exporting Countries, declares a punitive embargo on oil shipments to nations, including the United States, that supported Israel in its most recent war with Egypt. The OPEC oil embargo causes a sharp rise in gasoline prices and creates acute shortages and around-the-block lines at some filling stations in the United States.

OCTOBER 20 — President Nixon commits the "Saturday night massacre." With his hold on the White House becoming increasingly untenable, Nixon orders Attorney General Elliot Richardson to fire Watergate special prosecutor Archibald Cox. Richardson refuses and resigns. When Richardson's second-in-command, Deputy Attorney General William Ruckelshaus, also refuses to fire Cox, President Nixon fires Ruckelshaus. The president finally calls on U.S. Solicitor General Robert Bork, a staunch conservative, who does fire Cox. Cox had insisted that President Nixon turn over tape recordings of Oval Office conversations, refusing to accept the transcripts Nixon offered instead of the tapes themselves.

OCTOBER 23 — Eight resolutions of impeachment are introduced in the House of Representatives almost simultaneously with President Nixon's announcement that he will turn over the White House tapes subpoenaed by

Congress. On November 1, the president also appoints a new special prosecutor, Leon Jaworski, and pledges to refrain from interfering with the investigation.

NOVEMBER 7 — Congress overrides President Nixon's veto of the War Powers Resolution, which sharply curtails the president's ability to make war by requiring that Congress approve all armed commitments greater than 60 days in length.

1974

JULY 30 — The House Judiciary Committee votes three articles of impeachment against President Nixon. Nixon releases transcripts of his tapes on August 5, which reveal that he had directly and deliberately impeded the Watergate investigation. Three days later, on August 8, Richard Milhous Nixon becomes the first president in American history to resign, and Gerald R. Ford, whom Nixon had appointed vice president after the resignation of Spiro T. Agnew, immediately assumes the presidency.

SEPTEMBER 8 — President Gerald R. Ford announces a preemptive pardon of Richard Nixon for crimes he committed or may have committed while in office. While some welcome this as a necessary step toward national healing, others condemn it as evidence of a backroom deal between Ford and Nixon, who had appointed Ford to the vice presidency.

NOVEMBER 21 — The Freedom of Information Act, passed over President Ford's veto, provides broad public access to government files and allows citizens to challenge secrecy classifications in court.

1975

APRIL 26 — South Vietnam's president Tran Van Huong resigns, turning over power to Gen. Duong Van Minh, who, on April 29, surrenders to the North Vietnamese, thereby ending the Vietnam War. As North Vietnamese forces prepare to take Saigon, the capital of South Vietnam, the few remaining American ground troops in-country, all U.S. Marines, begin a frenzied helicopter evacuation of U.S. embassy personnel and certain South Vietnamese. At 12:15 p.m. the North Vietnamese flag is raised over Independence Palace, and Saigon is immediately renamed Ho Chi Minh City.

SEPTEMBER 5 AND SEPTEMBER 22 — President Ford is the target of two assassination attempts. The first, on September 5 in Sacramento, California, ends as a Secret Service agent wrests a handgun from Lynette A. "Squeaky" Fromme, a member of the "Manson Family," the cult of Charles Manson, who had directed the brutal murders of Sharon Tate and six others on August 6, 1969. In the second attempt, in San Francisco on September 22, Sara Jane Moore manages to fire at the president but misses. She is revealed as a deranged police and FBI informant.

SEPTEMBER 28 — Congress passes a law authorizing women to enroll in the nation's military service academies.

NOVEMBER 20 — A Senate committee led by Idaho's Frank A. Church reports that the FBI and CIA routinely conduct illegal surveillance of U.S. citizens and that the CIA has plotted to assassinate foreign leaders.

1976

APRIL 22 — Barbara Walters becomes the first woman to anchor a network television news program, co-hosting with Harry Reasoner on the ABC evening news. Accepting a $5 million five-year contract with ABC, she also becomes the highest-paid journalist, male or female, up to that time. (In September 2006, Katie Couric, long-time co-host of the *Today* morning program, leaves NBC to become anchor of the *CBS Evening News* at a yearly salary of $15 million.)

SEPTEMBER 30 — California passes the nation's first "right-to-die" law, granting adults the right to authorize a physician to disconnect life-support devices when death is imminent.

NOVEMBER 2 — Democrat Jimmy Carter is elected president, defeating Gerald R. Ford by a modest margin, 40,828,929 to 39,148,940.

1977

JANUARY 21 — President Carter issues a blanket presidential pardon to virtually all Vietnam-era draft resisters.

SEPTEMBER 7 — In a controversial act, President Carter signs a pair of new Panama Canal treaties, turning the canal and the Canal Zone over to Panamanian sovereignty.

1978

JANUARY 6 — The Wampanoag Indians of Mashpee, Massachusetts, lose a suit to recover 13,700 acres of Cape Cod, setting a precedent for similar cases brought by Indian tribes, mostly in the Northeast.

JUNE 28 — In *University of California* v. *Bakke,* the Supreme Court rules that the university violated the civil rights of Allan P. Bakke, a white man, by refusing to admit him to medical school because the school's quota of white students had been filled. The court effectively rules racial quotas unconstitutional, even when they are used in affirmative action programs to increase minority enrollment.

AUGUST 7 — The federal government declares the land and community around the Love Canal in Niagara Falls, New York, an environmental disaster area and orders an evacuation and resident compensation. The Love Canal had been used as a dump for toxic waste from 1947 to 1952.

NOVEMBER 18 — Jim Jones, leader of the People's Temple, a religious cult that has moved from California to a compound in the jungles of Guyana, is inspected by a delegation including U.S. Representative Leo J. Ryan and others. Apparently fearing that Ryan will expose abuses among the cult, Jones orders the murder of Ryan and other visitors, then leads the mass suicide, mostly by poisoning, of 911 cult members, including more than 200 children. Jones commits suicide him-self, by gunshot.

NOVEMBER 27 — Mayor George Moscone and City Supervisor Harvey Milk of San Francisco are shot to death in City Hall by former supervisor Dan White. Milk was a promi-nent leader of San Francisco's gay community, and White had resigned as city supervisor after passage of a gay rights bill that he had opposed. At his trial, White's lawyers suc-cessfully use what the media dubs the "Twinkie defense," citing White's massive and uncharacteristic consumption of Twinkies and other junk food as evidence of his pro-found depression when he committed the crime. (Some media outlets mistakenly report that the defense offers the consumption of Twinkies as the *cause* of the depression and, therefore, the cause of the crime.) White is convicted of voluntary manslaughter rather than murder and serves five years in prison before he is paroled. Angry protests sweep the San Francisco gay community after pronounce-ment of the "light" sentence. White commits suicide two years after his release from prison.

DECEMBER 15 — In the culmination of a process that began with President Nixon's meeting with Chairman Mao Zedong during February 21–28, 1972, the People's Republic of China and the United States announce the establishment of full diplomatic relations. The normaliza-tion goes into effect on January 1, 1979, and the United States ends its recognition of Taiwan, which had broken away from China during the Communist revolution.

1979

THE UNITED STATES settles an important Indian land claim suit by paying the Sioux nation $17.5 million for a portion of the Black Hills appropriated from the Sioux in 1877.

FEBRUARY 8 — The United States cuts back its ties to the repressive regime of Anastasio Somoza DeBayle of Nicaragua, ending military support and reducing economic aid. Up to this point, the United States has supported the Somoza family because of the family's opposition to leftist influences in the country.

MARCH 26 — President Carter brokers a momentous peace treaty between Egypt and Israel, signed at the White House by Prime Minister Menachem Begin of Israel and President Anwar el-Sadat of Egypt.

MARCH 28 — A malfunction at the nuclear power plant at Three Mile Island, near Harrisburg, the Pennsylvania state capital, creates a minor release of radiation into the atmosphere and threatens to develop into a nuclear disaster of enormously destructive proportions. Ultimately, the problem is contained; however, it is clear that workers initially mishandled the situation, safeguards did not function properly, and power company officials misled state officials as well as the public as to the seriousness of the emergency. The near-disaster at Three Mile Island proves to be a total disaster for the United States nuclear power industry, which goes into sharp decline as new projects are aborted and planned projects scrapped under public pressure.

APRIL 3 — Jane Byrne is elected mayor of Chicago. Her victory, by a wide margin, makes her the first woman mayor of the "Second City."

JUNE 18 — The United States and Soviet Union sign the SALT II Strategic Arms Limitation Treaty. The treaty significantly reduces the numbers of nuclear and thermonuclear weapons allowed in the arsenals of the two nations; however, in response to the Soviet invasion of Afghanistan in 1980, President Carter asks the Senate to suspend ratification. Although the treaty is never ratified, both sides use it as a guide to mutual arms limitation.

NOVEMBER 4 — Militant Iranian "students" seize the U.S. embassy in Tehran and take 90 hostages, including 66 American nationals. They release the non-Americans and 13 American women and black hostages, but the rest are held for the balance of Carter's term in the White House, in apparent revenge for Carter having allowed the shah of Iran into the United States for treatment of his terminal cancer. The Iran hostage crisis destroys whatever chance Carter has for reelection, and it drags on, day after day for 444 days, as a major American humiliation.

DECEMBER 21 — Congress approves a federal bailout of the ailing Chrysler Corporation, providing $1.5 billion in loan guarantees. The loans are repaid and, thanks in large measure to Chrysler's dynamic chairman, Lee Iacocca, the company becomes profitable once again.

1980

MARCH 17 — President Carter signs the Refugee Act of 1980, which broadens the definition of "refugee" to include persons from virtually anywhere. The ceiling on the number of refugees to be admitted to the Untied States is raised from 290,000 to 320,000.

APRIL 24 — A daring mission to rescue the Iran hostages, authorized by President Carter, fails when three of eight helicopters required for the mission suffer mechanical problems. A fourth helicopter collides with a C-130 transport, killing eight and injuring five.

MAY 18 — Mount St. Helens erupts in southwestern Washington State. This major volcanic eruption kills 57, destroys about 120 square miles of forest, and triggers fires, mudslides, and floods.

NOVEMBER 4 — Republican Ronald Reagan—a former governor of California (1966–1974), movie actor, television personality, and General Electric pitchman—is elected president, defeating incumbent Jimmy Carter by a wide margin, 42,797,153 to 34,434,100. Benefiting from Reagan's message of economic rebirth, Republicans attain a Senate majority and also gain House seats, but remain in the minority there.

DECEMBER 8 — John Lennon, formerly of the Beatles, is murdered in New York by a crazed fan, Mark Chapman. At the time of his death, some revere Lennon more than any contemporary political or religious leader.

1981

JANUARY 20 — The Iran hostage crisis ends with the release of the hostages on the day of President Reagan's inauguration.

FEBRUARY 18 — President Reagan delivers his first State of the Union Address and calls for a spectacular cut of $41 billion in President Carter's proposed budget. He also proposes a 10 percent cut in personal income tax in each of the next three years and more liberal rules governing business tax deductions for depreciation. Collectively, these measures form the basis of "Reaganomics," which proponents say will "jump start" the stagnant economy, but which opponents claim will cause great hardship among the poor and working class (the cutbacks are heaviest in social services areas) and will create unacceptable budget deficits, especially because Reagan has also announced a $5 billion increase in defense spending.

MARCH AND JUNE — Eight cases of an uncommon skin cancer called Kaposi's sarcoma, usually found in the elderly, appear in young gay men in New York City. During this same time, physicians note an increase in the number of cases of a rare lung infection, *Pneumocystis carinii pneumonia*. In June, the Centers for Disease Control publishes a report on these phenomena, which is generally viewed as the beginning of an awareness of the disease later called Acquired Immune Deficiency Syndrome (AIDS). The U.S. government is slow to respond to an epidemic widely misperceived to be caused exclusively by gay sex.

MARCH 30 — In an attempted assassination, President Reagan is shot by John W. Hinckley. Also wounded are White House press secretary James Brady, Secret Service agent Timothy J. McCarthy, and Washington Metropolitan Police officer Thomas K. Delahanty. The 70-year-old Reagan demonstrates extraordinary courage and grace in the aftermath of the shooting and during his recovery from a wound in the left lung. He returns to the White House on April 11. Brady never fully recovers from serious brain damage. Hinckley, who wanted to kill the president apparently in order to impress the young actress Jody Foster, is found not guilty by reason of insanity and committed to St. Elizabeth's Mental Hospital in Washington.

APRIL 4 — Henry Cisneros is elected mayor of San Antonio, Texas, the first Mexican-American mayor of a major American city.

APRIL 12–14 — *Columbia*, the first space shuttle, flies a successful three-day mission. The crew consists of Robert L. Crippen and John W. Young. The space shuttle is the first reusable spacecraft and is intended to make space travel more or less a matter of routine.

AUGUST 12 — IBM introduces the IBM PC. The "PC" stands for "personal computer," and it describes a device that puts at least some of the power of a room-size "mainframe" computer on a desktop. The new product enjoys only moderate success at first, but, within a few years, revolutionizes the workplace as well as the home.

SEPTEMBER 25 — Sandra Day O'Connor becomes the first woman appointed to the Supreme Court.

1982

JUNE 8 — In a speech to the British House of Commons, President Reagan calls the Soviet Union an "evil empire." The U.S. diplomatic corps and others are shocked, fearing the damage the remark will do to U.S.–Soviet relations; however, contrary to common sense, those relations actually improve.

JUNE 30 — The proposed Equal Rights Amendment dies when it fails to achieve the required 38-state ratification, despite the extension Congress has granted it. Only 35 states had ratified it.

SEPTEMBER 29 – OCTOBER 1 — Cyanide-laced Tylenol pain-reliever capsules kill seven persons in the Chicago area. James Burke, the CEO of Johnson & Johnson, the maker of Tylenol, immediately recalls all Tylenol from store shelves nationwide. Far from harming Johnson & Johnson or the reputation of Tylenol, this step enables the rapid rehabilitation of the product and its reissue in "tamper-resistant" packaging. In an era marked by many instances of corporate greed and misconduct, Burke's action stands as an example of lofty public ethics.

DECEMBER 2 — Barney C. Clark, age 61, receives the first successful artificial heart implant in an operation performed at the University of Utah Medical Center. Dr. William DeVries implants a Jarvik-7 artificial heart, designed by Dr. Robert Jarvik. Clark, whose death is imminent at the time of the surgery, survives for 112 days. America and the world are excited by this advance in "bionic medicine," although further results with artificial hearts prove disappointing for long-term survival and acceptable quality of life.

1983

SEPTEMBER 23 — Employees save their jobs by buying out the failing Weirton Steel Works in West Virginia. It is the biggest employee buyout in U.S. history.

OCTOBER 23 — In Lebanon, 241 U.S. Marines and sailors are killed when a suicide bomber drives an explosives-packed truck into the marine barracks in Beirut, capital of the civil war–torn country. All U.S. forces are withdrawn from the troubled region in 1984.

OCTOBER 25 — U.S. forces invade the small Caribbean island nation of Grenada after its government is toppled

U.S. POPULATION: 227,259,000

by a pro-Cuban Marxist coup. The island is declared secure on November 2, after some 1,100 U.S. nationals, mostly students at a local medical school, have been safely evacuated. Nineteen U.S. military personnel are killed and 116 wounded. Cuban forces lose 25 dead, 59 wounded, and 45 Grenadan military personnel are killed, another 250 wounded. Critics of President Reagan condemn the invasion as a blatant attempt to draw national attention away from the disastrous terrorist attack, just two days before, on marines in Beirut. Supporters, however, point out that the operation has successfully rescued imperiled American citizens and is in keeping with the long-time Cold War policy of the United States to keep the hemisphere free of new Communist nations.

1984

MOTOROLA INTRODUCES the DynaTac 8000X, the first commercial cellular telephone. Weighing in at about two pounds, the DynaTac is aptly nicknamed "the brick." Its price, $3,995, puts it well beyond the mainstream market, but by 2005, there will be 2.14 billion cell phone subscribers worldwide.

NOVEMBER 6 — Ronald Reagan is reelected in the greatest Republican landslide in history, defeating Democrat Walter F. Mondale (whose running mate, Geraldine Ferraro, the representative from New York's Ninth District, is the first woman nominated by a major party as a vice presidential candidate) 54,455,075 to 37,577,185 and carrying every state except Mondale's native Minnesota and the District of Columbia.

1985

JANUARY 18 — The United States withdraws from World Court proceedings brought against it by Nicaragua, which charges the United States with conducting a covert war in aid of rebel *contra* forces (whom President Reagan calls "freedom fighters") fighting to overthrow the leftist Sandinista government. On October 7, the U.S. Department of State announces that it will no longer automatically comply with decisions of the World Court, arguing that the court has become politicized.

DECEMBER 12 — President Reagan signs the Gramm-Rudman-Hollings Act, mandating the elimination of the federal deficit by 1991. The law obliges the president to make automatic spending cuts if Congress fails to meet each year's deficit ceiling; however, Social Security, interest on the national debt, and certain programs for the poor are exempted from cuts.

1986

JANUARY 28 — The space shuttle *Challenger* explodes 74 seconds after liftoff, killing all seven astronauts aboard, including Christa McAuliffe, a schoolteacher who had been chosen as the first private citizen to fly in the shuttle. Subsequent investigation shows that the accident is the result of the failure of an "O-ring" seal on a solid-fuel booster rocket, a failure NASA knew was possible but, apparently to avoid further delays in an already repeatedly delayed launch, chose to downplay as an acceptable risk.

MAY 27 — President Reagan abrogates the U.S.–Soviet SALT II nuclear arms reduction agreement. Because of the 1980 Soviet invasion of Afghanistan, President Carter had suspended ratification of SALT II; however, the two nations continued to abide by the unratified agreement. Although President Reagan declares that the nation will no longer consider itself bound by the agreement, he announces, also on May 27, the dismantling of two Poseidon guided-missile submarines to make way for a new Trident submarine, a step that is squarely in line with the provisions of SALT II.

NOVEMBER 3 — A Lebanese magazine reports that the United States has been secretly selling arms to Iran in the hope that this will secure the release of U.S. hostages held in Lebanon. On November 13, President Reagan admits knowledge of the sale, but, on November 25, he denies *full* knowledge of the operation. On November 25, the nation learns that profits from the sale of arms to Iran, a terrorist nation and sworn enemy of the United States, were used to finance the *contras* in their war against the Sandinista government of Nicaragua. The "Iran-Contra Affair" was carried out without the knowledge or authorization of Congress. Vice Adm. John M. Poindexter, Reagan's national security adviser and an architect of Iran-Contra, resigns, and his chief aide, Marine Lieutenant Colonel Oliver L. North is dismissed. A congressional investigation is launched into a scandal that some predict will result in the impeachment of President Reagan in what many now call "Irangate," echoing the Watergate scandal that ended the Nixon presidency. On November 18, 1987, Congress issues its final report, concluding that the president bears ultimate responsibility for the Iran-Contra Affair. North and Poindexter are indicted on March 16, 1988, and each is convicted on several counts, all of which, however, are subsequently overturned. In the meantime, on June 27, 1986, the World Court rules in favor of Nicaragua in the case of *Nicaragua v. United States,* but the United States refuses to pay restitution, vetoes a UN resolution calling on all states to obey international law, and ignores a General Assembly resolution calling on the United States to pay restitution. In the end, President Reagan escapes from the Iran-Contra Affair mostly unscathed, a feat for which the press dubs him "the Teflon president," since nothing seems to stick to him.

1987

MARCH 19 — The enormously popular and influential "televangelist" Jim Bakker resigns his ministry in disgrace when it is revealed that he is an adulterer and has paid a former lover (a church secretary) for her silence. Shortly after Bakker's tearful televised mea culpa, he is charged with 24 counts of fraud and conspiracy for embezzling millions of dollars in assets belonging to his evangelical empire. Convicted on 23 counts, he is sentenced to prison for 45 years. The sentence is later reduced on appeal to 18 years, and Bakker is paroled on July 1, 1994.

In June 2003, he returns to the airwaves with a brand-new television ministry, *The New Jim Bakker Show.*

APRIL 16 — The United States authorizes the award of patents for new forms of life created through gene splicing.

JUNE 12 — In a speech at the Brandenburg Gate and the ugly wall that has divided East and West Berlin throughout the Cold War, President Ronald Reagan rhetorically addresses Mikhail Gorbachev, leader of the Soviet Union: "General Secretary Gorbachev, if you seek peace, if you seek prosperity for the Soviet Union and Eastern Europe, if you seek liberalization: Come here to this gate! Mr. Gorbachev, open this gate! Mr. Gorbachev, tear down this wall!" By the fall of 1989, East and West Berliners begin physically chipping away at the Berlin Wall, and the border is effectively opened on November 9, 1989, symbolically ending the Cold War and signaling the impending collapse of Eastern European and, ultimately, Soviet Communism.

OCTOBER 19 — "Black Monday," the worst crash in the history of the New York Stock Exchange, results in a one-day loss of 508 points in the Dow Jones average, representing 22 percent of its value—almost double that of the 1929 crash that ushered in the Great Depression. Banking and other financial regulations not in place in 1929 prevent another freefall, and the underlying soundness of the economy, beleaguered though it is, staves off anything approaching another Great Depression.

1988

MARCH 14 — The U.S. Senate ratifies a multinational treaty to protect the Earth's ozone layer. The treaty requires developed nations to freeze and then roll back the manufacture and use of chlorofluorocarbons (CFCs), including aerosol propellants and most popular refrigerants—substances shown to damage the ozone layer, which protects the Earth from excessive exposure to ultraviolet radiation from the sun.

NOVEMBER 8 — George H. W. Bush, the vice president under Ronald Reagan, is elected president, defeating Democrat Michael Dukakis by a substantial margin: 47,917,341 to 41,013,030. However, Democrats increase their majorities in the Senate and House.

1989

FEBRUARY 3 — In an era characterized by corporate raiding, leveraged buyouts, and "mega-mergers," the investment firm of Kohlberg Kravis and Roberts (KKR) agrees to acquire the tobacco and food giant RJR Nabisco for $25 billion. It is the largest takeover in world business history.

MARCH 24 — The supertanker *Exxon Valdez* runs aground in Prince William Sound, Alaska, disgorging 240,000 barrels of crude oil. The worst oil spill in American history, it kills or menaces wildlife (some 400,000 animals) over 730 miles of pristine Alaskan shoreline. Though the Sound has proved resilient in recovery, serious effects remain to this day.

AUGUST 9 — President George H. W. Bush signs a law to bail out the nation's ailing savings and loan associations to the tune of $300 billion over a ten-year period, using, for the most part, tax revenues. The "thrifts," as these S&Ls are also called, had made bad loans or dangerous investments or had even engaged in outright criminal activity.

DECEMBER 20 — Operation Just Cause is launched: 24,000 U.S. service personnel, invade Panama for the purpose of capturing its strongman president, Manuel Antonio Noriega, who has been indicted by a U.S. court for drug trafficking. Noriega surrenders on January 3, 1990. Operation Just Cause costs 23 Americans killed and 323 wounded, while the Panama Defense Forces lose an estimated 314 killed and 124 wounded. Some 200 Panamanian citizens are also killed. Noriega is sentenced to 40 years in prison on September 16, 1992.

1990

APRIL 25 — The space shuttle *Discovery* launches the Hubble Space Telescope. Although a flaw is discovered in the telescope's mirror on June 25, a subsequent space shuttle mission repairs it, and Hubble transmits to Earth hundreds of thousands of images of deep space without the atmospheric interference that severely limits even the largest earthbound telescopes. Thanks to Hubble, astronomers observe extrasolar planets (planets outside of our solar system) for the first time and acquire data revealing much about the very origin of the universe.

Hubble stands as one of the greatest achievements in the history of science.

JULY 26 — President George H. W. Bush signs the Americans with Disabilities Act (ADA), forbidding discrimination in employment, housing, and public accommodations against persons with disabilities.

1990–1991

AUGUST 2, 1990–FEBRUARY 27, 1991 — Operations Desert Shield and Desert Storm are conducted with the object of removing Iraqi invaders from Kuwait. The operations constitute the First Persian Gulf War, which is waged against Saddam Hussein's Iraq by a United Nations–sanctioned international coalition led by the United States. Iraq suffers a massive military defeat and Kuwait is liberated, yet Saddam Hussein remains in power after the war.

1991

OCTOBER 15 — Clarence Thomas, a conservative African-American nominee to the Supreme Court, is narrowly confirmed by the Senate after he is accused of sexual harassment by Anita F. Hill, a black woman who is a law professor and a former Thomas aide.

NOVEMBER 21 — President Bush signs the Civil Rights Act of 1991, which facilitates employment discrimination lawsuits by shifting the burden of proof from employee to employer.

1992

FEBRUARY 1 — George H. W. Bush and Russian leader Boris Yeltsin proclaim an end to the Cold War in a joint statement issued in Washington, following new agreements reducing and limiting the two nations' nuclear arsenals.

MARCH 4 — An infertility specialist, Dr. Cecil B. Jackson, is convicted in Virginia on 52 counts of fraud and perjury for artificially inseminating patients with his own sperm. At least 15 children were fathered in this way (although the prosecution charges as many as 75). The case, which illustrates an ethical danger inherent in artificial insemination and related fields, is typical of the new moral and legal challenges posed by recent scientific progress.

JUNE 12 — President George H. W. Bush addresses the Earth Summit in Rio de Janeiro, Brazil, and announces that the United States will not sign the International Ecological Treaty, which most of the other 172 nations at the summit have already pledged to sign. He claims the treaty, which provides for the protection of rare and endangered species, will retard technology and "undermine the protection of ideas." As a result of the failure to sign the treaty, many in the world community regard the United States as an ecological pariah.

AUGUST 24 — Hurricane Andrew ravages southern Florida with 150-mile-per-hour winds, damaging or destroying 85,000 homes and leaving 250,000 homeless. Thirty-eight persons are killed, and damage is estimated at $30 billion. It is the most powerful recorded storm in U.S. history.

NOVEMBER 3 — Democrat Bill Clinton is elected president, defeating incumbent George H. W. Bush, widely regarded as having failed to improve an underperforming U.S. economy. Clinton captures 43,728,375 votes versus 38,167,416 for Bush. Industrialist H. Ross Perot polls an impressive third-party showing of 18,237,247 votes.

1992–1994

DECEMBER 1992 — President George H. W. Bush launches Operation Restore Hope in Somalia, seeking to aid the starving population of a country without a legitimate government and at the mercy of competing warlords. President Bill Clinton continues the operation, which, in an environment of anarchy, proves futile. On October 3, 1993, an elite unit of U.S. Army Delta Force commandos, aboard army Black Hawk helicopters, swoops down on Mogadishu, Somalia's capital, to capture Mohamed Farah Aided, the most powerful and vicious of the warlords. The unit is overwhelmed by local militia forces, and the 15-hour "Black Hawk Down" siege ensues, in which 18 U.S. soldiers are killed. American television audiences witness horrific scenes in which the mutilated body of one soldier is dragged through the dusty streets of Mogadishu. Public reaction revolts against Operation Restore Hope, which is brought to an end on March 25, 1994, with the withdrawal of all U.S. forces from Somalia. It is a bitter lesson about the limits of what even a superpower can do in the world.

1992–1995

THE UNITED STATES intervenes in the Bosnian Civil War, which pits Bosnian Catholic Croats and Bosnian Muslim Slavs against Bosnian Orthodox Serbs. The war develops in the wake of the dissolution of Communist Yugoslavia and is characterized by much atrocity on all sides. Throughout the war, the United States and other nations attempt to broker peace. In April 1994, the United States launches air strikes against Serb positions in Bosnia. At last, the Clinton administration manages to bring all sides to a series of conferences held at Wright-Patterson Air Force Base outside of Dayton, Ohio, and, on December 14, 1995, Bosnian Slav, Croat, and Serb leaders sign the Dayton Peace Accords, ending the war.

1994

JANUARY 1994 — After years of controversy, the United States, Canada, and Mexico launch the North American Free Trade Agreement (NAFTA), creating the world's largest free trade area. The object of NAFTA is to remove trade barriers and thereby stimulate trade among the three nations, but critics charge that it will result in a substantial net loss of U.S. jobs. More than a decade after the launch of NAFTA, the debate continues over its effect on jobs; however, encouraged by what he deems the success of NAFTA, President George W. Bush signs into law on August 2, 2005, CAFTA—the Central American Free Trade Agreement—

which creates NAFTA-like free trade between the United States and six Central American nations.

1995

APRIL 19 — Domestic terrorism strikes the United States when a truck packed with an explosive manufactured from nitrate fertilizer detonates at the Alfred P. Murrah Federal Office Building in Oklahoma City, killing 168 persons, including children at play in the building's daycare center. Timothy McVeigh and Terry Nichols, two disaffected U.S. Army veterans, are indicted and tried. McVeigh is found guilty in June 1997 and sentenced to death; he is executed on June 11, 2001. Nichols, found guilty on December 23, 1997, of involuntary manslaughter and of having conspired with McVeigh, is sentenced to life imprisonment. Both men are associated with the "militia movement," a phrase that describes militant groups organized in several states in self-proclaimed opposition to what they identify as federal tyranny, particularly as exemplified in two recent incidents: the 1992 ten-day federal siege of the armed compound of white supremacist Randy Weaver—wanted on weapons charges—and his family in Ruby Ridge, Idaho (in which a deputy U.S. marshal and Weaver's son, wife, and dog were killed), and the April 19, 1993, FBI raid on the illegally armed "Branch Davidian" communal compound in Waco, Texas, in which 80 commune members, including 24 children, died (four federal agents had been shot to death in an earlier assault on the compound).

OCTOBER 3 — Following a spectacular nationally televised trial of 266 days, O. J. Simpson, a former football star turned sports broadcaster and all-around celebrity, is found not guilty of having murdered his ex-wife, Nicole Brown Simpson, and her friend Ronald Goldman on June 12, 1994. The jury has deliberated for just four hours, and its verdict reveals most dramatically the sharp racial divide that still exists in the United States at the end of the 20th century. Although Simpson's prosecutors present what they call a "mountain of evidence" against him, most African Americans, including those on the jury, believe his defense, that he is the innocent victim of racist police officers determined to frame him for the murder of his white ex-wife and her white friend.

1996

NOVEMBER 5 — President Clinton wins reelection as president, the first Democrat since Franklin D. Roosevelt to do so. Enjoying economic prosperity, Americans give Clinton a substantial victory over Republican challenger Bob Dole, with Clinton carrying 31 states and the District of Columbia and Dole just 19.

1996–1999

LESS THAN A YEAR after the end of the war in Bosnia, the Kosovo Liberation Army (KLA) launches a rebellion against the Federal Republic of Yugoslavia, of which Kosovo is a province. Slobodan Milosevic, president of

U.S. POPULATION: 249,632,692

the Federal Republic, conducts a brutal campaign to crush the rebellion, and a full-scale civil war breaks out, accompanied by many atrocities. President Clinton calls on NATO for a military response, and U.S. and other NATO forces mount the largest Allied military assault in Europe since World War II. Some 35,000 air sorties (mostly U.S.) are flown before Milosevic backs down on June 3, 1999, declaring acceptance of an international peace plan. On June 29, 2001, Milosevic is delivered for trial by a war crimes tribunal at The Hague, Netherlands.

1998

SEPTEMBER 11 — The Republican-controlled Congress publishes on the Internet the full text of a report written under the direction of Kenneth Starr, an independent counsel appointed to investigate allegations of possibly impeachable offenses committed by President Bill Clinton. (The product of four years of investigation at a cost of $40 million, the "Starr Report" details the president's sexual liaison with a 21-year-old White House intern, Monica Lewinsky. The report had begun as an inquiry into the involvement of Bill Clinton and his wife, Hillary, in a shady real-estate investment known as Whitewater. Failing to find evidence of wrongdoing in this area, Starr focused instead on the Lewinsky affair, concluding that Clinton had violated his oath of office by perjuring himself in a sworn deposition he had given in a sexual harassment civil lawsuit brought against him by a former Arkansas state employee, Paula Jones. It was also alleged that the president had lied about the Lewinsky affair to a grand jury.) Based on the Starr Report, Congress votes, along party lines, to impeach President Clinton, who is nevertheless acquitted on February 12, 1999, in a Senate vote also along party lines.

2000

JANUARY 1 — Anxiety over the "Millennium Bug" suddenly abates with the uneventful arrival and departure of the New Year. Throughout 1999, many Americans had been gripped by fear that the shorthand computer programmers had used during the 1960s and 1970s—expressing all years in two rather than four digits ("75" instead of "1975")—would create a kind of cyber Armageddon with the dawn of the new century, because computers would be unable to recognize "00" as the year 2000 and would see it instead as a rewinding of time to 1900. This "Millennium Bug" or "Millennium Bomb," it was widely predicted, would bring commerce, industry, banking, government, and transportation to a grinding and chaotic halt. As a result, a new multibillion-dollar industry briefly sprang up, as governments and private companies scrambled to employ armies of programmers to purge their extensive computer software of the bug. On January 1, 2000, however, it becomes clear that the Millennium Bomb is a dud. Some attribute this nonevent to a gross overestimation of the Millennium Bug problem, while others point to the success of feverish work by programmers.

DECEMBER 13 — Democrat Al Gore concedes the 2000 presidential election to Republican candidate George

W. Bush, son of former president George H. W. Bush. Gore had polled 50,996,116 popular votes against 50,456,169 for Bush, but a disputed result in Florida ultimately gave Bush a majority of electoral votes. Bush's popular margin in Florida, a state governed by his younger brother, Jeb, was a razor-thin 1,784 votes over Gore. A legally mandated recount shaved the Bush lead to just 327 votes. Democrats demanded a further recount by hand in four counties where they had reason to believe significant numbers of Gore votes had not been counted. This led to a tortured attempt to evaluate thousands of questionable punch-card ballots. As legal representatives of the two candidates battled for days over the recount of questioned ballots, Democrats also pointed to another flaw in the election process, a confusing ballot in Palm Beach County, which led many (especially elderly voters) to cast their ballot unintentionally for right-wing extremist Patrick J. Buchanan instead of Gore. Amid suits and counter-suits, Katherine Harris, Florida's secretary of state, declared her intention to certify Bush as the winner on the legal deadline for certification, November 14. Harris, the state's top election official, had served as a Bush delegate to the Republican National Convention and was one of eight cochairpersons of the Bush campaign in Florida. Ultimately, the dispute was carried through the Florida Supreme Court to the U.S. Supreme Court, which, on December 12, by a five-to-four vote, barred all further manual recounts, leaving Bush the winner in Florida by 537 votes.

2001

JANUARY 11 — In an eagerly watched megadeal, America Online (AOL), flagship of "dot-com" companies, acquires Time Warner, the world's largest media company. The explosive development of personal computers and the Internet had culminated in the 1990s dot-com boom, a frenzy among investors to invest in (it seemed) any company doing business on the Internet and therefore having a name ending in ".com," the suffix of most World Wide Web commercial addresses. Within two years of the AOL–Time Warner marriage, the CEOs who made the deal are driven out and, in October 2003, the company drops "AOL" from its name. The change is symbolic of the sudden transition from dot-com to dot-bomb, as the vast majority of start-up dot-coms fail because of poor business plans, leaving investors high and dry and ending the long bull market and economic boom that have characterized most of the Clinton years.

FEBRUARY 15 AND 16 — The scientific journals *Nature* (February 15) and *Science* (February 16) publish the first analyses of "maps" of the human genome, the genetic blueprint of the human organism. Mapping the human genome provides science with revolutionary new ways to understand human life and provides an entirely new way to understand, diagnose, and treat disease.

SEPTEMBER 11 — At 8:45 a.m. (EDT), a Boeing 767 passenger jet-liner (later identified as American Airlines

Flight 11 out of Boston) crashes into the north tower of the World Trade Center in Lower Manhattan. As TV cameras cover this unprecedented disaster, at 9:03, a second 767, United Airlines Flight 175, hits the World Trade Center's south tower. At 9:43, American Airlines Flight 77 plows into the Pentagon, headquarters of the U.S. military. Two minutes later, the White House is evacuated. In New York, at 10:05, the south tower of the World Trade Center collapses. Five minutes after this, United Airlines Flight 93 crashes in rural Somerset County, Pennsylvania. At 10:28, the north tower of the World Trade Center collapses. In the meantime, President George W. Bush, who had been visiting a Sarasota, Florida, elementary school classroom during the attacks, is flown from one "secure location" to another, finally returning to the White House shortly before 7 p.m., by which time the 47-story Building 7 of the World Trade Center has also collapsed. Before the end of the day, the media reports that U.S. officials believe that Osama bin Laden, a Saudi multimillionaire sponsor of terrorism living under the protection of the radical Islamic Taliban government in Afghanistan, is behind the attacks as leader of al Qaeda (Arabic for "the Base"), an Islamic guerrilla organization dedicated to fighting a *jihad*—a holy war—against Israel, the West, and the United States. Al Qaeda had sent 19 suicide hijackers to board the four planes, take them over, and transform them into highly destructive guided missiles. In the end, the death toll at the World Trade Center is fixed at 2,893—added to 189 killed at the

Pentagon (including the 64 passengers and crew of Flight 77) and 44 killed in the Pennsylvania crash. That aircraft, it is later learned, had been headed for the Capitol, but was downed as passengers struggled with the terrorist hijackers.

OCTOBER 4 — U.S. health officials report that a Florida man has contracted anthrax—the first case in the United States since the 1970s. He dies on October 5. Three days later, a second instance of exposure is discovered, then a third on October 10. On October 12, it is announced that an employee of NBC News, the personal assistant to the popular network news anchor Tom Brokaw, has been infected. The source of all of these infections, it is discovered, are letters laced with dry anthrax spores—the anthrax bacillus deliberately "weaponized." By the end of October, at least 40 persons are found to have been exposed, and a few become ill. One anthrax-laced letter reaches the office of Senate Minority Leader Tom Daschle, and on October 17, 31 Capitol workers (including 23 members of Daschle's staff) test positive for anthrax exposure. The Capitol and several Senate and House offices are temporarily shut down. The tainted letter (or perhaps some other piece of tainted mail) has also contaminated a Washington, D.C., postal facility, fatally infecting two postal employees. After it is announced on October 23 that anthrax spores have been detected in an army base facility that screens White House mail,

U.S. POPULATION: 282,339,000

President George W. Bush tells a press conference, "I don't have anthrax." But Americans are left wondering if the anthrax attacks are part of the same terrorist conspiracy that has brought down the World Trade Center and hit the Pentagon. The source of the anthrax letters has yet to be found.

OCTOBER 7 — American bombers and missiles attack targets in Afghanistan in an effort to remove the extremist Islamic Taliban government, which supports and harbors Osama bin Laden and his al-Qaeda, the man and organization identified as responsible for the September 11 terrorist attacks on New York and Washington. The war in Afghanistan is also aimed at finding bin Laden himself. The air strikes are coordinated with indigenous anti-Taliban ground forces (including the principal force known as the Northern Alliance) and with a small number of American special forces. Kabul, the Afghan capital, falls to the Northern Alliance on November 13, and a friendly government is installed on June 19, 2002, led by Hamid Karzai, who later (December 7, 2004) is elected president. As of late 2006, Osama bin Laden remains at large, and fighting in Afghanistan continues against what appears to be a resurgent Taliban.

OCTOBER 11–12 — The Senate (October 11) and House (October 12) pass the USA PATRIOT Act, anti-terrorist omnibus legislation providing measures against money laundering to finance international terrorism; immunity against prosecution for the providers of government-requested wiretaps; expanded systems of personal identification, especially at ports of entry into the United States; a foreign student monitoring program; a mandate to improve passports and other government-issued documents to prevent forgery; and provision for so called "Sneak-and-Peek" searches, authorizing surreptitious search warrants and seizures; expanded provisions for wiretaps and surveillance; and even the authority to examine library records to determine who is reading what. Highly controversial, the act is nevertheless renewed by Congress in 2006.

2003

February 1 — For the second time in NASA (National Aeronautics and Space Administration) history, a space shuttle meets with disaster: *Columbia* breaks up while reentering the Earth's atmosphere. The cause is a design flaw that allows foam insulation to perforate the shuttle's wing. Seven astronauts die, and the tragedy renews criticism of NASA's safety policies and calls into question the continued scientific value of the space shuttle.

MARCH 17 — President George W. Bush issues an ultimatum to Saddam Hussein, president of Iraq, demanding that he and his inner circle (including his sons, Uday and Qusay Hussein) permanently leave Iraq within 48 hours. When this deadline passes, on March 19, Bush authorizes a "decapitation" attack on the Iraqi leadership, an aerial bombardment of a bunker in Baghdad believed to shelter Saddam. This begins Operation Iraqi Freedom, the second war with Iraq. Starting in 2002, the president had attempted to garner broad international support for a war against Iraq, arguing that Saddam Hussein possessed weapons of mass destruction. In contrast to his father, George H. W. Bush, who created a very substantial military coalition against Saddam Hussein in 1990-1991, George W. Bush encountered much resistance in the international community to the proposed war, especially as definitive proof of the existence of the weapons of mass destruction was never found. (It is later concluded that the weapons did not exist.) The first phase of the war, an invasion, proceeds rapidly, and on April 14, 2003, the Pentagon announces that the major combat phase of Operation Iraqi Freedom is at an end. On July 22, Uday and Qusay Hussein are killed in a raid, and on December 13, 2003, Saddam Hussein himself is captured, having hidden in a hole near his birthplace, Takrit. Yet, as of late 2006, the war continues, as American and modest British forces, as well as forces of a U.S.-supported Iraqi government, combat both an insurgency (apparently consisting of pro-Saddam loyalists and terrorists from neighboring and more distant countries) as well as intense violence between the nation's Sunni and Shiite rival religious factions.

2004

FEBRUARY 4 — The Massachusetts Supreme Judicial Court declares that gay couples have a constitutional right to full, equal marriage, not just "civil unions." On February 12, city officials in San Francisco, California, begin issuing marriage licenses to homosexual couples and perform the first known civil marriage of a homosexual couple in the United States, marrying lesbians Del Martin and Phyllis Lyon. More than 80 other couples are given quick ceremonies. On February 24, President Bush announces his intention to support a constitutional amendment to ban same-sex marriage.

OCTOBER 27 — In St. Louis, the Boston Red Sox shut out the St. Louis Cardinals, 3–0, in game 4 of the World Series, thereby winning the club's first Series since 1918. Long-suffering Boston fans are jubilant, proclaiming an end at last to the "Curse of the Bambino"—an 86-year Series drought supposedly brought on by the 1920 sale of Boston's Babe Ruth ("the Bambino") to the New York Yankees. (In October 2005, the Chicago White Sox sweep the Houston Astros in four games to win the World Series, breaking an 88-year drought of their own.)

NOVEMBER 2 — Although some pundits predict that the increasingly unpopular war in Iraq will prevent it, George W. Bush is reelected president, defeating Democratic challenger John Kerry by 1 percent of the popular vote, a greater margin than even most Bush supporters had anticipated.

2005

MARCH 31 — Terri Schiavo dies at 9:05 a.m. in Florida. In 1990, the 27-year-old Schiavo had suffered cardiac arrest and slipped into a coma. Thereafter, she was fed through a feeding tube for nourishment and hydration. After her physicians declared her to be in a "persistent vegetative state"—effectively brain dead—Schiavo's husband, Michael, and her family disputed over removal of the feeding tube. The Schiavo case was argued in the courts beginning in 1993, Michael Schiavo seeking to remove the feeding tube, her parents seeking to keep it in place. During 2003, the argument escalated through the appeals courts, and Florida governor Jeb Bush, brother of President George W. Bush, intervened against Michael Schiavo. When state and federal courts repeatedly upheld Michael Schiavo's right as his wife's guardian to remove the feeding tube, Congress, shortly after 12:30 a.m. on March 21, 2005, passed a "private bill" to grant Schiavo's parents the right to continue suing for the maintenance of the feeding tube and to order reinsertion of the feeding tube while the suit was pending. It was signed by President Bush at 1:11 a.m. A federal district court refused to order the tube reinserted, however, the U.S. Supreme Court refused to hear the parents' appeal, and, amid much controversy and rancor, Schiavo slipped away. The case highlights an ongoing controversy between those advocating a right to "die with dignity" and those advocating what President Bush calls a "culture of life" (which often extends to sustaining life at virtually any cost as well as opposing contraception and abortion).

AUGUST 29 — Hurricane Katrina, a Category 4 storm with winds up to 145 miles per hour, makes landfall at 6:10 A.M.

local time, on August 29, near Buras, Louisiana. The eye of the storm narrowly misses a grateful New Orleans, but, on August 30, two of the city's flood walls give way, rapidly inundating some 80 percent of this below-sea-level city, in some areas to a depth of 20 feet. The massive hurricane cuts a broad swath of devastation along the Gulf Coast, including Biloxi and Gulfport, Mississippi, and Mobile, Alabama, as well as scores of smaller communities. The nation has been watching this storm develop since August 24, and New Orleans mayor Ray Nagin had ordered the city evacuated on August 28; however, the evacuation relies on citizens providing their own transportation, and perhaps 100,000 lack cars or other means of escape. Worse, local, state, and especially federal disaster relief is delayed for days as survivors cling to balconies and rooftops or swelter in makeshift shelters at the New Orleans Superdome and convention center. Privation, hunger, thirst, looting, and even civil insurrection ensue before the National Guard begins to arrive in numbers on September 2. With a final death toll of at least 1,836, Katrina proves less deadly than the Galveston (Texas) hurricane of September 8, 1900, but the estimated value of damages, $81.2 billion, makes it the costliest natural disaster in U.S. history. For many, Katrina also raises profound questions about social justice and racism in America (overwhelmingly, the victims who could not evacuate are African American and poor), America's apparently increased vulnerability to the effects of natural disaster and terrorist attack, and the nation's environmental policies.

2006

MAY 25 — Kenneth Lay, former chairman and CEO of Enron is found guilty of 10 counts of securities fraud, wire fraud, and making false and misleading statements in connection with the implosion of the once high-flying Houston-based energy trading firm. The massive corporate scandal had begun unraveling on November 8, 2001, when company officials admitted to overstating earnings for the past four years to the tune of about $586 million and of having failed to state liabilities amounting to some $3 billion in obligations to various partnerships. Enron had seemed a great American success story, an example of what deregulation—a government hands-off policy advocated most powerfully by Ronald Reagan in the 1980s—could achieve. The company made fortunes for highly placed employees and for investors; however, it had done this by means of massive deceit, effectively trading with itself through a maze of partnerships so that losses could be posted as apparent profits by passing expenses off to a "partner." (On July 5, 2006, Lay dies of a heart attack, three months before his scheduled sentencing. On October 17, a federal judge sets aside the conviction because Lay has had no opportunity to appeal.)

U.S. POPULATION: 300,000,000

Printed by the National Geographic Society
John M. Fahey, Jr., *President and Chief Executive Officer*
Gilbert M. Grosvenor, *Chairman of the Board*
Nina D. Hoffman, *Executive Vice President, President, Books and School Publishing*
Kevin Mulroy, *Senior Vice President and Publisher*
Marianne Koszorus, *Design Director*
Gary Colbert, *Production Director*
Lawrence M. Porges, *Project Editor*
Peggy Archambault, *Art Director*
Mike Horenstein, *Production Project Manager*
Cameron Zotter, *Production and Design Assistant*
Jack Brostrom, Rebecca Gross, Lynsey Jacob, Amy T. Jones, *Contributors*

Library of Congress Cataloging-in-Publication Data
Axelrod, Alan, 1952-
   1001 events that made America : a patriot's handbook / Alan Axelrod.
     p. cm.
   Includes index.
   ISBN 0-7922-5307-8
   1. United States--History--Chronology. 2. United States--History--Miscellanea. I. Title:
One thousand events that made America. II. Title: One thousand and one events that
made America. III. Title.
   E174.5.A98 2006
   973.02'02--dc22

                         2005056166

Founded in 1888, the National Geographic Society is one of the largest nonprofit scientific and educational organizations in the world. It reaches more than 285 million people worldwide each month through its official journal, NATIONAL GEOGRAPHIC, and its four other magazines; the National Geographic Channel; television documentaries; radio programs; films; books; videos and DVDs; maps; and interactive media. National Geographic has funded more than 8,000 scientific research projects and supports an education program combating geographic illiteracy.

For more information, please call
1-800-NGS LINE (647-5463)
or write to the following address:

National Geographic Society
1145 17th Street N.W.
Washington, D.C. 20036-4688 U.S.A.

Visit us online at www.nationalgeographic.com/books

For information about special discounts for bulk purchases, please contact
National Geographic Books Special Sales: ngspecsales@ngs.org

First Printing February, 2006

Paperback edition 2007, ISBN-10: 1-4262-0021-8; ISBN-13: 978-1-4262-0021-2

Printed in Mexico